D0153913

"For business leaders, investing in a more sustainable ecoɪ thing to do; it's the key to long-term business success. statistics and storytelling, Alice Mann brings this point t a seasoned professional, a budding entrepreneur, or an individual committed to tackling the great challenges of the world, *Future First* is a must-read."
— **Willy Foote**, Founder/CEO of Root Capital

"With her keen business acumen and deep compassion for people who will inherit our successes and failures, Mann has written a book that's one-part business strategy, one-part inspiration, and one-part plea to the leaders of the world to consider the long-term consequences of our actions. With *Future First*, Mann moves the corporate responsibility conversation forward by positioning social issues and global environmental degradation not as problems but innovation challenges. This is truly a must-read for any entrepreneur interested in achieving lasting and integrated business results and social change."
— **Kirsten Saenz Tobey**, Founder and Chief Impact Officer of Revolution Foods

"Mann's book should be required reading for any leader considering big changes in their company, or more importantly for any leader who isn't. *Future First* breaks down the barrier between profit-driven enterprises and environmental do-gooders. They can—and should—be one and the same."
— **Mark R. Tercek**, President and CEO of The Nature Conservancy and author of *Nature's Fortune*

"Renewable energy produces about 20% of the world's energy; sales of electric vehicles and organic produce are the fastest selling segments in their industries— *Future First* is an insightful and robust guidebook to how businesses can further accelerate this transformation to a sustainable economy."
— **Nancy Pfund**, Founder of Double Bottom Line Partners and early investor in Tesla Motors, SolarCity and Revolution Foods

"With her framing of the Five Practices of Future First, together with case studies of some of the leading firms working to integrate those practices into their business, Mann offers not only a window into the marketplace of tomorrow, but important insights into how today's CEOs and managers may best position themselves to shape that future. Given her years of experience consulting to leadership teams in diverse industries, she is able to offer both relevant lessons and compelling stories of how Future First Companies is a powerful framework for today's entrepreneurs and leadership teams."
— **Jed Emerson**, Author of *The Impact Investor: Lessons in Collaborative Capitalism* and Founder of BlendedValue.org

"Move over, 'Shared Value' and 'CSR': Here comes Alice Mann with *Future First*. This book is a well-written, deeply-researched analysis of businesses that have not just managed but embraced society's biggest challenges. Mann has sketched out a playbook to take companies beyond doing less harm to effecting meaningful change, with inspiring stories of the individuals making it happen."
    – **Christine Bader**, Author, *The Evolution of a Corporate Idealist: When Girl Meets Oil* and former Director, Social Responsibility, Amazon

"Mann convincingly shows in *Future First* that a new massive wealth opportunity is at our fingertips linking sustainability and economic development."
    – **Jigar Shah**, Co-Founder, Generate Capital

"Alice Mann nails it. A must read for First-Movers and companies concerned with staying on the forefront of innovation."
    – **Rebecca Costa,** American Sociobiologist and Author of *The Watchman's Rattle*

"Alice Mann has written a very exciting book. She offers leaders and their companies a practical path to a future where they can succeed by balancing profit and purpose. It turns we can 'do well by doing right,' and *Future First* shows us how."
    – **Erika Andersen,** Founding Partner of Proteus International and Author of *Be Bad First*

"In an era defined by short-termism, leaders who understand how to embrace global challenges as opportunities for sustainable innovation will gain a critical competitive edge. With her keen business acumen and deep compassion for the people who will inherit our successes and failures, Mann has written a book that's one-part business strategy and one-part inspiration for global leaders to consider the long-term consequences of our actions. *Future First* is an important and timely book."
    – **Ari Wallach,** Founder of Longpath and *Fast Company Futures*

Future First

Future First is a practical guide for any business leader who wants to build, expand, or reinvent their company by finding new value in global challenges. Traditional companies often view issues like income equality, global warming, and resource scarcity as "problems." By contrast, future first leaders understand them as opportunities, as innovation challenges.

Through real-life business examples ranging from Nike to Opower, this book lays out how to identify and adopt the future first leadership mindset and business capabilities required to achieve lasting and integrated performance results. *Future First* examines how leaders from companies including Unilever, Etsy, Revolution Foods, Method Products, and others have adopted this mindset toward innovation and people practices, accelerating business ecosystem transformation.

Alice Mann, an organizational psychologist with twenty years of experience consulting and coaching on executive leadership, organization design, and business transformation, interviewed scores of business leaders to understand how their companies are expanding into new value frontiers. *Future First* makes a convincing argument that successful partnerships and alliances among big global companies and small mission-driven ones can reshape the global ecosystems of apparel, food, automobiles, and energy, and remake the future of our world.

Alice Mann is founder of Mann Advisors, Senior Consultant at Kates Kesler Organization Consulting, Forbes.com Leadership columnist, and Lecturer at Columbia University, USA.

Future First

How Successful Leaders Turn Innovation
Challenges into New Value Frontiers

Alice Mann

Routledge
Taylor & Francis Group

LONDON AND NEW YORK

First published 2018
by Routledge
2 Park Square, Milton Park, Abingdon, Oxon OX14 4RN

and by Routledge
711 Third Avenue, New York, NY 10017

Routledge is an imprint of the Taylor & Francis Group, an informa business

British Library Cataloguing-in-Publication Data
A catalogue record for this book is available from the British Library

Library of Congress Cataloging-in-Publication Data
A catalog record for this book has been requested

ISBN: 978-1-78353-805-8 (hbk)
ISBN: 978-1-78353-763-1 (pbk)
ISBN: 978-1-351-26208-8 (ebk)

Typeset in Times New Roman
by Swales & Willis, Exeter, Devon, UK

For Sebastian, Julian, and Stella. I love each of you with my whole heart.

And for everyone's children, now and for many generations to come.

Contents

Contents

Introduction

Winning at the value frontier of the future

Toward the end of the last century, the ninety-three-year-old chairman of Toyota Motors, Eiji Toyoda, expressed a fundamental concern about his company's business. "What," he asked, "is the future of the automobile?"[1]

Toyoda wasn't talking about two or three years down the road. His company was already one of the largest car manufacturers in the world. Instead, the aging patriarch was asking something much more profound about the future relationship between cars and the environment. Toyoda wanted to build an environmentally friendly car capable of 47.5 miles per gallon. This was a ridiculously high number at the time; the high economy Corolla got about half that number.

The project, which became known as G21, for global twenty-first century, did not move forward smoothly. Engineers initially proposed technology to gain improvements from a conventional internal combustion engine. But the team eventually decided that they had to take an experimental drivetrain technology and turn it into a real car driven by real people. The hybrid car would be a much tougher path, but engineers thought it answered all the demands of Toyoda's G21 project: oil depletion, dirty emissions, and the long-term future of cars. Over the next few years, engineers worked through various major problems.

Fast forward to the release of the Prius. Within a year, it was obvious that Toyota was ahead of the game. Once the cars were in the showrooms, drivers were drawn to the novel technology. At the 2003 Academy Awards, Harrison Ford and other stars arrived in chauffeured Priuses. The funny-looking car was cool. Then fuel prices began to shoot upwards, making the Prius's fuel economy very attractive. Suddenly, Americans were demanding more cars than Japan could produce. US sales of the Prius roughly doubled in both 2004 and 2005.

Perhaps the ultimate vindication for Eiji Toyoda's vision came from his competition. At the 2004 North American Auto Show, GM's vice president of product development, Robert Lutz, dismissed hybrid technology as a "curiosity" that GM had no plans to compete with. And yet, just one year later, GM had announced plans to develop a hybrid with BMW; Audi had introduced the first European hybrid; and Porsche, Volkswagen, and DaimlerChrysler were scrambling to get their versions out. "I think," said a chastened Lutz, "the manifest success of the Prius caused a rethink on everyone's part."[2] People love to talk about "disruptive" technologies—a picture of the Prius should be next to the dictionary definition.

Toyoda's efforts were a prime example of future first leadership. The Prius gave the whole Toyota brand an environmental glow, but it wasn't a typical corporate sustainability effort. Likewise, future first decision-making is about much more than saving money on incremental energy and transportation efficiencies. It's bigger than appealing to environmentally conscious consumers with green products. And not every future first success story plays out on such a grand stage; in fact, most don't.

Take, for example, Samasource, a business that connects impoverished people around the world with digital work. CEO and founder Leila Janah, a Harvard-trained management consultant, became disillusioned with the work she had been doing at the World Bank.[3] So, in 2008, she started Samasource with funding from Silicon Valley investors. Sama means "equal" in Sanskrit, and the company got onto Fast Company's top most innovative companies list in 2016.

One of the company's innovations is proprietary software that breaks digital work from clients, such as Google and Walmart, into smaller pieces. These smaller bits can then be efficiently farmed out to workers from the slums of Nairobi or Haiti or even rural Arkansas. The other side of Samasource's success is a three-week training program that develops workers who may have never owned a computer to do technical work like flagging content on TripAdvisor or improving Google search algorithms.[4]

Samasource will never have the same profile as a mainstream product like Prius, but by creating a new model for fighting poverty, it has had a significant impact on the lives of tens of thousands of people. It also allows larger, traditional companies to participate in an innovative, future-leaning development project. In this sense, a new kind of social enterprise can be just as important an innovation as the Prius.

What is future first?

Future first companies get ahead of the pack by innovating within the limits of commercial success while making a net positive material impact on the world's biggest challenges. They play by the rules of profitability and business growth, but with a twist. Their positive impact comes from reducing harm and scaling benefits to the environment and people's lives.

What distinguishes future first leaders is that regardless of the size of their company, the size of their vision and the scale of their impact are large enough to remake the markets and industries where they play. Future first innovation transforms entire business ecosystems, like food, cars, energy, clothes, and technology, because it happens through a network of exchange among big and small companies, and their investors, partners, competitors, and customers.

No matter what kind of company you run, or are a part of, there's an advantage to having a future first mindset. You want to be a leader. You want to be out in front of the trends affecting your company's ability to create all kinds of value over the next ten to fifteen years. But when everybody is racing to get to the same place, the question changes from "What do *you* want your company to become?"

to "How can you discern future trends *before* they happen? How do you discover *new* value frontiers?"

The world is too dynamic to predict exactly what will happen a decade or two from now. But future first leaders are embracing the big innovation challenges affecting the entire private sector today. The biggest challenges we face are the ones I tackle head-on in this book: climate change, resource scarcity, and social dynamism, since they are certain to affect our global economy for a long time. Climate change from a hotter planet will push the private sector to accelerate solutions in clean energy, manufacturing, and transportation. Growing scarcity in water, land, and other natural resources will challenge whole industries, like apparel and agriculture, to come up with new materials and means of production. Social dynamism from the changing demographics and values of the global workforce and consumers will push companies to redefine how people work, eat, travel, and live.

These forces will inevitably and fundamentally remake entire industries. We've seen small hints of what's to come. For instance, nine Atlantic hurricanes occurred in a row in 2017, unprecedented in their frequency and size. These extreme weather events took human lives, left millions of homes without clean water or electricity, and will cost the public and private sector hundreds of billions of dollars. The North American ski industry is being wiped out by warmer winters, electrical failures in burgeoning Indian cities have left 700 million people and businesses without power for days, and there have been targeted military strikes on dams, bottling plants, and water infrastructure across the parched Middle East.

On the face of it, these are grim, even hopeless, problems. But future first companies recognize that accepting and engaging the world's biggest challenges is the key to unlocking new forms of value. Winning at the new value frontier of the future starts by getting out ahead of tomorrow's demands and opportunities for innovation. These types of businesses, from Tesla Motors to Patagonia to Unilever, are winning by identifying these trends in advance of others. Their responses to these huge problems have been qualitatively different from that of many other top corporations. Future first leaders realize that these global challenges aren't going away soon, and the demands created by them will only grow for many decades to come.

What future first leaders and companies have in common is a profound commitment to two or more of these five business practices: (1) they are *embracing sustainability as an innovation challenge* by designing commercially successful products, production processes, and people practices, within certain environmental and social limitations; (2) they are *overcoming presentism* by combatting our culture's profound tendency to capture our attention in the here and now, and instead they are tuning into future trends that drive long-term value; (3) they are *developing integrative thinking* by creating solutions that synthesize the best of seemingly opposing ideas, and thereby reduce the limitations of polarized thinking; (4) they are *expanding the values that drive their business decisions*, by being transparent and well-reasoned about all the values that inform their decision-making; (5) they are going *beyond one-company, one-leader at a time* by providing solutions to global problems outside of the narrow scope of their sectors and outside the confines of their company walls.

Why I wrote this book

As an organizational psychologist, I know firsthand the challenges that companies face when they aim to make a positive difference in the world. For the last ten years, I have consulted on and researched what future first companies do differently to generate profitable, scalable, and lasting solutions for people and the planet. I got excited about the difference that business can make in the world early in my career when I worked at a small investment firm in San Francisco called Hambrecht and Quist (H&Q) during the late 1990s. H&Q underwrote the IPOs of companies like Apple, Genentech, Netscape, and Amazon. I came to H&Q somewhat reluctantly because of my preconceived notions about how staid and uninspiring the investment world would be. But my assumptions were quickly stood on their head when I saw my colleagues investing in cutting-edge technology companies with the promise to change the world.

When H&Q was sold to Chase in 1999, I was surprised to discover how much I loved being out in front of big organizational changes. A couple of years later, I was leading restructuring efforts during the JPMorgan Chase merger. When the Chase acquisition of Bank One was announced in 2004, I moved to New York City to develop a global operating model for 10,000 people in the technology department. At the same time, I earned my MA and PhD in social and organizational psychology at Columbia University.

As much as I enjoyed my stint as VP at JPMorgan Chase, I was eager to go out on my own so I could apply everything I had learned in both the corporate world and in graduate school. Once the merger with Bank One began settling down in 2005, I left the bank and launched my own consulting business. I quickly gravitated toward working with purpose-driven organizations. Just as I had been surprised by how much inspiration and fun there was in the financial services industry, I was equally surprised by how much reluctance there was to prioritize revenue generation and efficient business processes in mission-driven organizations. Fascinated by how the competing goals of profit and purpose affected every aspect of these organizations, I wrote my doctoral dissertation on the topic.

I had learned from experience to hold the big companies, like JPMorgan and my corporate clients, in high regard for being places where people got things done quickly and profitably. But six months after giving birth to twin boys, I was astonished by hearing about the collapse of Lehman Brothers and Bear Stearns on the news. The stories left me in utter disbelief. How could this happen in an industry with so many smart people? Just as I was bringing new life into the world, the economy and financial sector seemed to be falling apart.

I kept searching for solutions to the world's biggest problems in the private sector. But I could only find a handful of big and small companies that had cracked the nut of creating profitable businesses that maximized their net material positive impact at anywhere near the scale the world needs. The young purpose-driven companies were aiming to do *more good* by scaling innovative solutions to big social and environmental problems. In contrast, the big corporate giants that had been around for decades were seeking to do *less bad* by innovating new products and services and production processes.

As I continued to dig, I discovered that the cross-pollination across ecosystems between the small and mid-sized companies that were nimbly incubating new solutions and business models, and the big companies leveraging their scale to demand more sustainable supply chain and people practices, was the most fertile ground for solving the world's biggest challenges. Despite all of the heroic efforts to build more sustainable and socially impactful companies large and small, global warming, resource scarcity, and social dynamism are on the rise. This made me wonder: *How could I help more business leaders and innovators like you expand or transform your company to be future first, and fast?*

This question became all the more urgent to me after my daughter was born. Once I became a mother of three, my sense of responsibility for the next generation's future only grew fiercer. When Superstorm Sandy hit in 2012, the pole carrying electrical wires to our home just north of New York City snapped in two and ripped another electrical pole off the side of our house. As the stories poured in of more than 230 people dead,[5] over 650,000 homes destroyed or damaged, and 8 million people without power,[6] I waited with two toddlers and a baby for fourteen days to get our electrical poles, wires, and transmitters replaced. Gas station lines grew longer and people got more panicky. In the US we assume the infrastructure that provides our electricity and petrol on demand will always be there for us. It was a wake-up call to me when I considered how many more extreme weather events like these would be part of ours and our children's futures. Already, we have seen more devastating hurricanes, floods, wild fires and droughts since Superstorm Sandy.

While I was writing this book, I became quite unexpectedly divorced. Suddenly, my future entailed the greater economic and social risks that come with being a single mother of three elementary school-age kids, something I never thought would happen to me. As I struggled to adjust to my new situation during that time, another realization hit home: I was now living in a reality that I had extensively researched before.

In graduate school, I had participated in a research study funded by the National Science Foundation (NSF) to look at why more women aren't at the top of most fields of science. The study found that tenure track scientist positions—like the top spots in almost all powerful industries—are more attainable for men than women. This is not because of any inherent differences in abilities, but because the career path has been designed for men in traditional gender roles and families. Now that I was juggling clients and kids as a single mother (not to mention writing this book!), my previous thinking about gender inequality in the workplace and home was confirmed by my own experience.

In this book I will be talking about the "old power economy," which refers to the tall pyramid structure of our existing economy—one that accrues vastly disproportionate levels of economic and social power typically to male bread-winners who are in traditional gender roles and families that mostly consist of heterosexual, white, two-parent households. (This dynamic can be confirmed somewhat less scientifically by looking at the photos accompanying the Forbes 2017 list of the World's Billionaires and counting the number of faces of women or faces of men of color.) The old power economy has two major shortcom-ings. Obviously, it perpetuates growing economic and social inequality for most people. But it is also rapidly becoming unsustainable for companies that need to tap into the global talent pool of the future—and it's certainly unsustainable for families and communities like mine.

Recently, a colleague invited me to propose a project with her to a very suc-cessful private equity firm. The firm wanted help figuring out how to get more women promoted to partner. The founders saw their challenge as a business prob-lem, not a gender problem. To us, the answer was obvious: The founders were financially successful white men with stay-at-home wives, or wives who worked in part-time or flexible jobs. As a result, the founders had designed their partner track around assumed traditional gender roles and a traditional family model that allowed them to devote the majority of their waking hours to building the firm and their relationships with each other and their clients, while leaving the majority of the unpaid (and let's face it, lower status) labor of taking care of their children and homes to their spouses.

If the private equity firm's founders wanted to get serious about promoting women to partner, they would have to redesign the partner track, not just for mothers, but for single parents, and fathers with full-time working spouses, and really for anyone who wanted to or needed to be consistently taking care of chil-dren, other family members, and their homes.

Business leaders with an eye on hiring and promoting the talent of the future will go further than just hiring more men of color and women into lower- and mid-level jobs and hoping they will figure out how to make it on their own. They will redesign the most powerful jobs and the career paths to the top of their companies and industries to grow the future value of what I call in this book the "new power economy." In the new power economy, everyone—regardless of race, ethnicity, age, gender, sexual orientation, and parental or caretaker status—can contribute economically and socio-emotionally both to the companies where they work and to their families and communities.

My determination and drive to write this book came from my growing con-viction that the most essential solutions to our global challenges will come from harnessing the unprecedented power of the private sector. We can direct the enormous stake we all have in the future toward building and sustaining more successful future first companies. Business leaders, who care as much as any of us about the next generation's future, have a tremendous opportunity to lead the private sector toward future first solutions. All of our children's futures are at stake in the choices we make today and over the next decade.

Navigating the many paths of future first companies

I researched hundreds of companies for this book by looking for the most innovative and sustainable companies in the world. I drew from the Corporate Knights Top 100 Sustainability 2016 list, the 2015 Sustainable Leaders Report, the Fortune 1000 list, *Forbes*'s and *Fast Company*'s most innovative companies, the B-Corp awards, and the GameChangers: Top 500 list. I culled my list down to the 100 top companies that earn between $20 million to over $200 billion in annual revenue and demonstrate two or more future first business practices.

I went out and interviewed more than fifty business and thought leaders, including leaders from many of my top future first companies list. Some of these leaders work in big corporations, like Unilever, Nike, Samsung, Sony, and Ingersoll Rand. But I also talked with founders and investors in successful purpose-driven companies. Among them is Alex Laskey, Co-founder and Past President of Opower, which makes cloud-based software for the utility industry and was sold to Oracle in 2016. I spoke with Kirsten Tobey, Co-founder of Revolution Foods, which makes healthy affordable meals for urban school districts across the US. I interviewed Adam Lowry, Founder of Method Products, whose green cleaning supplies can be found in major supermarkets, and Matt Stinchcomb, one of the first employees of Etsy. I also talked with Nancy Pfund, Founder of DBL and an early investor in Tesla Motors and SolarCity.

Future first leaders understand that they gain enormous advantages from getting out ahead of future trends and expanding, transforming, or reinventing their companies to solve the world's biggest challenges. The future first companies I feature in this book are not only adopting future first practices, they're adopting a future first leadership mindset and baking these practices into their companies' DNA.

Future first companies start with the mindset and conviction of their leaders. These are a new class of leaders. They are not scared off by how fast the world is changing. They are clear-sighted and think for themselves. They care deeply about the future of the world and the well-being of the next generation. They bring a whole new mindset to business. If you are among these leaders, or you want to be, this book is for you.

Notes

1 Taylor, A. (2006, February 24). The birth of the Prius. *Fortune*. Retrieved from http:// archive.fortune.com/magazines/fortune/fortune_archive/2006/03/06/8370702/index.htm
2 Ibid.

3 Kessler, S. (2016, February 16). Sama Group is redefining what it means to be a not-for-profit business. *Fast Company*. Retrieved from www.fastcompany.com/3056067/most-innovative-companies/sama-group-for-redefining-what-it-means-to-be-a-not-for-profit-bus
4 Ibid.
5 Diakakis, M., Deligiannakis, G., Katsetsiadou, K., & Lekkas, E. (2015). Hurricane Sandy mortality in the Caribbean and continental North America. *Disaster Prevention and Management*, 24(1), 132–148.
6 Rice, D. & Dastagir, A.E. (2013, October 29). One year after Sandy, 9 devastating facts. *USA Today*.

1 The power to change everything

When I was working at JPMorgan Chase in 2004, the CIO made a telling slip of the tongue while presenting the bank's annual technology budget. Instead of referring to the "*company*'s annual expenses," he called it the "*country*'s annual expenses." It hit me then how apropos his comment actually was. After all, we were spending more than the GDP of most small countries on technology alone. The leaders of that bank had the power of corporate kings.

With total assets of $2.42 trillion, JPMorgan Chase and Company is the largest bank in the US and the world's most valuable bank according to its market capitalization.[1] The bank's global conglomerate structure, which encompasses five subsidiaries, evolved from numerous mergers and acquisitions over the last twenty years, including the two I supported with Chase Manhattan Bank and Bank One. But the outsized national influence of JP Morgan, the man, is nothing compared to the global economic power of his namesake company and all its offshoots today.

Massive consolidation of economic power has become more the rule than the exception worldwide. This is true outside of the financial sector as well. In 2015, there were roughly 45,500 companies listed in public markets worldwide. Out of those, the top 500 largest global companies, or 0.01 percent, were responsible for nearly half of the $70 trillion of the total value of the global markets.[2] Within certain industries, such as financial services, transportation, energy, and agriculture, the power of a few huge corporations is extremely concentrated, and highly interconnected and distributed throughout the world. The globalized nature of today's markets not only gives large corporations power all over the world, but enormous leverage—and much larger budgets—than most countries.

The good, the bad, and the possible

All this global wealth and influence has presented corporations with a remarkable capacity to reshape societies and the environment. The results of this consolidation of power in the private sector have been mixed. Business and technological innovations should get much of the credit for the unparalleled rises in material wealth and lifespans over the past few hundred years. At the same time, this economic activity has produced a number of negative impacts, such as pollution and wealth inequality, at an unprecedented global scale.

Until relatively recently, it was easy to argue that, on a macro level, contemporary globalized corporate economies produced more positive impacts than negative ones. Pharmaceutical companies, for example, created drugs that saved lives, and improved the quality of countless millions more. Web-based companies provided new access to information and cultural resources. But, today, we are rapidly approaching a tipping point in which our most common ways of making things, providing services, and creating wealth are dragging us toward a crisis.

Admittedly, these sorts of claims have been made repeatedly, but this time it's different for several reasons. For one, the resistance to traditional corporate economies is coming from the left and the right. In the midst of all its nativism, cynicism, hyperbole, and theatrics, the outcome of the 2016 US presidential election was about an erosion of confidence in the political and economic center. Among the three top vote getters in the primaries—Sanders, Clinton, and Trump—one actively identified as a socialist while the winner repeatedly criticized virtually every institution in American society, vociferously attacking free trade agreements that have been at the core of global commercial expansion for more than two decades. In the UK, a similar dynamic had played out months earlier with the Brexit vote to withdraw from the European Union. Far right parties across Europe have ridden similar disillusionment to success in the polls, although the French election of 2017 took a notably different turn.

While certain indicators of economic health—most notably stock markets—are still at record levels, the current disenchantment with economic realities worldwide is certainly related to the 2007–08 economic crisis. Whatever complicated political passions shaped recent popular votes in the industrialized world, the fact is that GDP growth between 2008 and 2015 averaged an anemic 2.231 percent.[3] This is an historic downturn. As an article in the *New York Times* on August 6, 2016 put it: "Economic growth in advanced nations has been weaker for longer than it has been in the lifetime of most people on earth."[4] But some believe that the massive economic growth of the 20th century, boosted by two world wars and the explosion of the fossil-fuel energy market, is not repeatable, let alone sustainable.

Bringing externalities back inside

Companies set out to turn a profit, not to create global problems. But reviewing these global challenges is the preface for a pressing question: How do business leaders separate the positive impacts of for-profit business activity from the negatives?

One answer lies in the traditional accounting used by businesses, which is often able to make the negative impacts of a company's activity disappear. The invisible part is often referred to as "externalities," any costs *or* benefits created by commercial activity that affects a party who did not choose to incur them. A beekeeper, for example, gets a benefit if her hives are next to an orchard where the bees can feed. Likewise, a residence or commercial facility that runs on solar power puts renewable energy back into the grid for local electricity consumers to use instead of traditional electricity.

But externalities are most often discussed as net negatives. For example, the effluent that is produced by an industrial hog farm that runs into nearby rivers not only kills fish and plants, but also creates costs that include local cleanup efforts, lost revenue from commercial fishing or tourism, and a lower quality of life for people who live nearby. Externalities aren't limited to local issues either. A glass factory that burns large amounts of greenhouse gases contributes to global warming everywhere. Neither are externalities all environmental. Offshoring a call center will take a toll on the people and area where the jobs used to be, including increases in household debt, drops in consumer spending, and less local tax revenue.

Despite the wide range of costs that effluent runoff or offshoring customer service creates, none of them ends up on the spreadsheet. Accounting is limited to "internal" costs, like labor, marketing, research, HR, production, and the supply chain. Even if a company is aware of the "external" costs created by its activities, its accounting essentially says, "that's not my problem," and keeps those costs off the spreadsheet. But, in a world facing multiple crises, we no longer have the luxury to pretend that these costs to the environment and society aren't there. We can see them everywhere, from overfishing to the declining life expectancy among white Americans driven by anxiety-related drug abuse and suicide.[5]

If we want to create a more lasting and connected globalized economy, we need to stop treating pollution, inequality, resource scarcity, exploding populations, and so on as "problems" to be avoided. Companies must stop forcing these costly problems outside their bottom-line calculations. In fact, business must stop seeing them as problems altogether. They are, instead, challenges and innovating to solve them is the greatest growth opportunity of the foreseeable future.

Valuing transformation

Many businesses have realized the value in seeing global problems as innovation challenges. Pharmaceutical companies, for example, looked at the rapidly aging populations in the industrial world and created a slew of drugs to treat high cholesterol, macular degeneration, and enlarged prostates. Many businesses have adapted practices that reduce or eliminate externalities. Even global companies are not monochromatic. They can be part of a new economy that values so-called externalities in making business decisions.

JPMorgan Chase has paid out enormous sums of money for their involvement in huge corporate scandals like Enron and the subprime mortgage crisis, but it has also had a powerful hand in ventures that have had a positive impact on society. One of the bank's legacy companies, inherited through a merger, was Hambrecht & Quist (H&Q), a legendary investment bank where I once worked, known for its success in developing Silicon Valley companies like Apple, Adobe, and Amazon. H&Q pioneered the Bay Area Equity Fund, a social impact venture fund started in 1989 that was subsumed by the JPMorgan Chase merger in 2000, and was eventually spun off in 2008 to create DBL (Double Bottom Line) Partners, an early investor in successful innovators like Tesla Motors, SolarCity, and Revolution Foods.

Like many multinational companies, JPMorgan Chase has all kinds of positive impacts that have contributed in non-linear ways to the reduction of negative externalities in major industries like automobiles, energy, and food. In 2017, nearly 1 percent of new car sales in the US were for all-electric cars, and the cost of all-electric cars in the US is predicted to go down below the cost of gas cars by 2022.[6] Renewable energy sourced 20 percent of the global energy market, and that piece of the pie is only getting bigger.

Many corporate giants are using their unprecedented size and economic power to solve problems by setting standards for emissions reduction, increasing usage of clean energy, reducing reliance on toxic chemicals, and fairly treating and empowering a global workforce. From Walmart to Google, global companies are converting their power sources to renewable sources of energy because it makes financial sense. Multinationals, like Apple and Nike, are improving their transparency and standards for the fair treatment of workers in their outsourced factories. Other groups, from environmentalists to labor unions to more segmented philanthropies, have made huge contributions to rectify the damage created by business externalities.

And while these efforts are to be commended, they're still too slow. Traditional businesses too often choose to ignore many externalities, at least until they must face legal action or strikes. Too many companies still act as if externalities are not their problem.

Future first businesses, by contrast, realize that there are no true externalities, whether positive or negative. It is now clear that the earth cannot endlessly absorb pollution and population growth. Likewise, wages cannot continually be depressed by further offshoring; neither will foreign markets guarantee endless growth. There is a limit to things. "Externalities" always return, sometimes in the form of multi-billion-dollar lawsuits or damage to the value of companies' brands.

Facing unprecedented challenges, from our exploding population to climate change, we are racing against time. And because we need transformations in how businesses operate to happen faster and in a more widespread way, future first leaders are needed as well. These leaders come to the table with a new mindset that confronts externalities without recourse to regulation. They create business models that look beyond the immediate goal of producing a profitable product or service tomorrow. Their businesses survey the current and future material impacts of all their practices. A future first leader can clearly see the shortcomings of past business practices, but they don't want to make businesses any less powerful a force in the world. Instead they want to use their tremendous influence as a catalyst for positive change.

How change happens now

To update the rules of the global economy, we need new legal, financial, and business models, and new tools for business growth and transformation. Much of what is still taught in business schools—and adopted by business leaders and management consultants today—is outdated material made for early twentieth-century corporations. Not only does it use externality-based accounting, it is also a bad fit for the size, complexity, and reach of today's corporations.

These antiquated approaches assume that corporations are singular and self-contained systems with a central home base, limited global impact, and a few powerful leaders at the top who can campaign for change across the company. One of my clients was a multinational food corporation. The executive leaders' task was to redesign incredibly complex and interdependent global divisions—from marketing to IT and Human Resources—in collaboration with each other, while getting the rest of the company to follow along. Once they had coordinated their efforts across all their global functions and brands, they could translate their global operating model from two-dimensional PowerPoint slides into new ways of actually working together around the world.

Business transformation is a wholly different endeavor now than it was when the field of management began in the early 1900s. Companies of all sizes are embedded within vast complex networks of people, business and government partners, and technological and environmental systems. The individual agency of business leaders doesn't hold a candle to the power and complexity of the global systems in which they operate. Companies evolve now through technological innovation and competition with players of all sizes across markets and industries to transform whole ecosystems, like cars, food, and energy. Any major change in the material impact of business will have to match how companies actually do business today.

Picked by *The Economist* as one of the Top Ten Business Books of 2007, *Forces for Good*[7] is based on the extensive research that authors Leslie Crutchfield and Heather Mcleod Grant conducted on thousands of non-profit organizations to understand how top performers had the highest impact. They made the counter-intuitive discovery that the greatest impact did not come from focusing internally on the organization's growth or effective management. Rather, the highest impact came from working with and through other organizations and partners to amplify a non-profit's impact across a field and industry to a much greater extent than what it could do alone. Change, in other words, is a team effort.

But in the private sector, few business leaders deliberately seek to achieve broader goals across their industries and markets over time, which is why it's notable when a company extends its locus of control and influence beyond its company walls. As the largest corporation in the world, for example, Walmart employs 2.2 million people globally and makes more in annual sales than the GDP of all but the richest twenty-eight countries in the world.[8] By most measures, Walmart's practices are far from ideal. The company's record on fair treatment of employees is spotty at best. But in 2015 the company reported that it had reduced 28.2 million metric tons of greenhouse gases over the previous five years. This is equivalent to taking 5.9 million cars off the road for a year.[9] This was accomplished by finding a combination of efficiencies in its supply chain, including the way it loads trucks and how much fertilizer its produce suppliers use. The point of this story is not to laud Walmart's effort—it has made too little progress on other fronts, including purchasing green energy, and could not be considered a future first company. But their example shows how major change across a massive supply chain can occur.

It's important to note that the transformation of business practices is not solely the responsibility or domain of huge corporations. Younger, more agile businesses have an equally important role to play as innovators that can accelerate the rate of change and bring new solutions to the table. While multinationals like JPMorgan or Walmart can provide scale for deep transformations, smaller businesses can be the nimble incubators for the rapid reinvention of products and processes that will continue to redefine cars, food, water, energy, clothes, shopping, and other industries.

Finding value in transformation: Coca-Cola and the city too busy to hate

Although the need for transformation in business leadership has a new urgency now, companies have long used their enormous power to exert progressive change. In the early 1960s, Atlanta attempted to distance itself from racial strife and violence across the South. The mayor and other civic leaders branded Atlanta "The City Too Busy to Hate" in an attempt to remove the stigma of segregation from a city that wanted to be seen as an international commercial center. As part of the effort, the mayor hosted a dinner honoring Martin Luther King, Jr. in 1964, the year King received the Nobel Peace Prize. But many businesses, all of them white-owned, weren't on board from a values perspective and so they refused to buy tickets that supported Dr. King's powerful message of peace and anti-racism.

Desperate for Atlanta to be seen in a different light, the mayor eventually called on the city's largest and most iconic business, Coca-Cola, to help rally the reluctant members of the white business community to the cause. Coca-Cola's leaders made it clear that the other businesses in Atlanta needed them, threatening to leave if the community was going to be comprised of Civil Rights laggards. People listened to Coke. The event quickly sold out.[10]

More recently we have seen multinational companies protesting vehemently against the gendered bathrooms laws in North Carolina. Arguing that they can't recruit and maintain the best people with such bigoted laws in place, North Carolina-founded PepsiCo has been joined by an enormous list of companies, from Dow Chemical to American Airlines to Starbucks, in protesting against the law. Companies including Deutsche Bank and PayPal have cancelled planned expansions in the state. These actions have given huge support to the efforts of local leaders protesting against the bill. But this was not just a protest campaign; the corporations also saw the business value of standing up for the rights of their transgender employees in their efforts.

Here's the interesting thing about Coca-Cola's involvement in King's Atlanta speech: The company's arm-twisting didn't add traditional business value. But it wasn't just a charitable gesture either. Distancing itself from racial strife and choosing to come down on the right side of history spotlighted Coca-Cola's progressive values. By getting Atlanta's business leaders to respectfully attend an event with one of the city's most famous citizens, Coca-Cola was able to improve—or at least protect—the positive perception of the city associated with the soft drink brand. But ultimately Coca-Cola took a stand in favor of the people and the place of Atlanta, which promoted the values of the company more broadly and thus created goodwill and long-term business value.

Valuing innovation

We can look to the Coca-Cola story as a history lesson for today's business leaders who are asking the question: "How can business best use its tremendous power?" Coca-Cola found value in an unexpected place, by engaging one of the most pernicious social problems of the United States of America. Today, businesses can look for similar opportunities to embrace seemingly intractable national and global problems wherever they threaten the company's value or values.

Take, for example, resource scarcity or the tumult created by exploding populations and the resulting social dynamism that comes with the changing faces of the workforce population, who will ultimately be in power across global businesses. All these future trends are described by NGOs and national defense intelligence assessments alike as risks to social stability. But they are actually some of the best places to look for future value. However, pushing this value frontier requires a change in how leaders view the issues. A huge opportunity is growing to embrace the changing values that social dynamism brings to the workplace. The next generation of workers brings new values that reflect the changing attitudes, beliefs, and lifestyles of global cultures and customers. Business leaders who get out ahead of these future trends will examine and integrate new values in the way they do business and how they generate lasting business value.

Notes

1 Ausick, P. (2016, April 13). The world's largest banks. Retrieved from http://247wallst.com/banking-finance/2016/04/13/the-worlds-largest-banks/

2 Dullforce, A. (2015, June 19). FT 500 Introduction and methodology. Retrieved from https://www.ft.com/content/1fda5794-169f-11e5-b07f-00144feabdc0

3 The World Bank. (2017). GDP growth (annual %). Retrieved from http://data.worldbank.org/indicator/NY.GDP.MKTP.KD.ZG?end=2015&start=1961&view=chart

4 Irwin, N. (2016, August 6). We're in a low-growth world. How did we get here? *The New York Times*. Retrieved from www.nytimes.com/2016/08/07/upshot/were-in-a-low-growth-world-how-did-we-get-here.html?_r=0

5 Avernise, S. (2016, April 20). White Americans are dying younger as drug and alcohol abuse rises. *The New York Times*. Retrieved from www.nytimes.com/2016/04/20/health/life-expectancy-decline-mortality.html

6 Mitchell, R. (2016, Nov. 14). Electric cars are less than 1% of the market. Yet automakers are pushing them big time. Why? *LA Times*. Retrieved from www.latimes.com/business/autos/la-fi-hy-electric-car-future-auto-show-20161114-story.html

7 Crutchfield, L. & Mcleod Grant, H. (2007). *Forces for good*. San Francisco, CA: Jossey-Bass.

8 Synder, B. (2015, June 6). 9 facts about Walmart that will surprise you. *Fortune*.

9 Gunther, M. (2015, November 18). Walmart is slapping itself on the back for sustainability. *The Guardian*. Retrieved from www.theguardian.com/sustainable-business/2015/nov/18/walmart-climate-change-carbon-emissions-renewabe-energy-environment

10 Moye, J. (2015, January 14). The night Atlanta truly became the city too busy to hate. Retrieved from www.coca-colacompany.com/stories/the-night-atlanta-truly-became-the-city-too-busy-to-hate-

2 Embracing our biggest innovation challenges

Reconciling the 250 people who are born every minute with the finite resources of the planet will require enormous efforts of innovation. Tackling huge dynamics like exploding populations will never be successful without thousands or millions of different efforts. But these efforts will also not succeed with incremental improvements. In other words, seemingly intractable problems are the ultimate test of innovation. They force businesses to think creatively about huge challenges.

These challenges are not opportunities that are going away. Their worst feature, intractability, also guarantees a nearly limitless market for solutions. When a leader decides to innovate around the challenges of access to clean water or women's empowerment, it's like discovering a new continent full of possibilities.

But future first leaders don't just plunder the resources of this new continent. This sort of economic activity was practiced for centuries, a model that is distinctly un-innovative and, ultimately, unsustainable. Take the classic example of the imperial Spanish economy. Following its colonization of the Americas in the sixteenth century, the empire was flush with money from the extraction of gold and silver. But, though its elites were wealthy and its armies well funded, the Spanish economy was one-dimensional. High domestic prices made its exports uncompetitive, entrepreneurship was discouraged, and the nation's industrialization lagged far behind the rest of Western Europe. The inevitable result? Declining resource extraction followed by the American independence movements in the early 1800s left Spain adrift with a largely agricultural economic base. It took another century and a half—i.e. the 1970s—for the nation to reach modern European levels of industrialization.

But today a disproportionate amount of the economic growth that has occurred has been created by developing countries, most notably China. And China's rapid expansion over the past several decades now points to a different type of crisis. The country is suffering from pollution created by its super-charged economy. During red alerts, the air quality is five times worse than the level that is considered acceptable by global health authorities, compelling city officials to alternate daily bans on cars with even and odd license plates.[1] In addition to precipitating a health crisis, environmental devastation has polluted over 40 percent of China's arable land and created fears over the nation's ability to produce enough food to feed its enormous population. Perhaps even more immediately, the earth's growing populations are exhausting the supply of not just extractable resources, but drinkable water itself.

This is not just a Chinese problem. There is an overwhelming scientific consensus that the concentration of greenhouse gases in the earth's atmosphere is the main cause of an increasingly hot planet that will see a rise in severe weather events, forest fires, flooding, and droughts, among other climate fluctuations. The predictions, which have been largely accepted by governments and business communities, point toward extinction-level events. By 2020, the world will likely have lost two-thirds of its population of mammals, birds, fish, reptiles, and other vertebrates since 1970.[2] For many species, these population drops will become permanent.

The world is rapidly moving toward the first mass extinction since the dinosaurs disappeared 65 million years ago. The first mammalian causality of climate change, a rat native to an Australian island, has disappeared from the earth as of 2014. Its habitat was destroyed by rising sea levels, driven by climate change.[3] A dozen other animal species are already gone or are facing extinction, and up to half of the animal species on the planet in 2015 have been predicted to become extinct by 2100.[4] The thread linking all these negatives, from low growth to climate disaster to resource depletion, is that our way of doing business is crashing up against the realities of a finite earth with a growing population of humans.

At a fundamental level, all extraction-based economies face this same fate. Though future first leaders don't rely on this dead-end model, they still sometimes run a business that extracts natural materials from the earth. But any leader doing so today also recognizes that future value lies in massive innovation to solve global challenges, not exacerbate them. A lumber company might be pivoting toward supplying advanced recycling technology. An oil company might be transitioning toward cheap, power-dense batteries to store wind power more effectively. Such efforts will have net positive material impacts in the world, but they also provide value for a company. Innovating around inevitable global challenges has another name: future-proofing.

Innovation challenge #1: climate change

Scientists, climate researchers, and some politicians have been publicly warning about the dangers posed by the warming of the earth's climate since at least the 1980s. Their message is stark: Climate change poses a threat to nearly everything about how humans work, play, eat, and live. This is because, on our current trajectory, the average global temperature will rise 7.5 degrees Fahrenheit by the end of the century.[5] On a planet that much hotter, New York and other major coastal cities will likely either be underwater or surrounded by huge dykes. Infectious diseases now limited to tropical areas will proliferate globally. Droughts and floods will make contemporary farming techniques useless in many parts of the world.

Though it's not easy to think about, the phenomenon is also directly linked to our modern business practices. Companies burn unprecedented amounts of wood, coal, and petroleum products doing everything from producing and delivering physical products to cooling the server farms that enable internet activity. These materials, when burned, release huge stores of carbon dioxide. Carbon dioxide and other greenhouse gases like methane remain in the atmosphere trapping heat; the more greenhouse gases, the more heat they retain and the hotter the planet gets.

Because few countries in the world require corporations (or consumers for that matter) to pay for putting greenhouse gas emissions into the earth's atmosphere, climate change has no place on traditional accounting spreadsheets. In a sense, greenhouse gases are the ultimate externality—local economic activity creates global pollution that lasts for centuries. Faced with this challenge, companies and whole industries have taken numerous divergent paths. Some businesses—notably petroleum and energy companies—have spent a lot of time and money pushing back on the idea that human activity has anything to do with the rising temperatures.

Some businesses have had no choice but to adapt to the new conditions. Wine growers in Burgundy, for example, have been forced to adopt new varieties of grapes that can flourish in warmer summers—a near scandal in the proprietary, conservative world of French vintners.

Other companies have accepted the consensus that we have caused—and thus can slow—this global climate risk. What's more, they see embracing this innovation challenge as a competitive advantage. Steve Howard, IKEA's Chief Sustainability Officer, said that renewable energy will play a prominent role in his company's vision of the future. "The next decade's business is going to be shaped by who's really efficient, where they get sustainable raw materials from, and the way they make their products," said Howard, adding "Climate change is a biggie. That's why we're into renewable energy and expanding renewables in our supply chain as well."[6]

IKEA's efforts, which include rooftop solar electrical generation, are "just the right thing to do," said Howard, "but it also future proofs you. We make long-term business decisions. Most businesses don't, I think, really look that far ahead."[7]

Two-thirds of climate change effects today come from burning fossil fuels like coal, oil, and gas for electricity and transportation. Worth nearly $5 trillion by 2014 stock market values,[8] the fossil fuel industry is one of the most profitable and powerful industries in history. The industry is highly subsidized by the top twenty richest countries in the world, and it has trillions of dollars' worth of oil reserves in the ground, much of which cannot be burned without destroying the planet. Our world economies and governments are inextricably tied to oil and gas companies, and it will take extraordinary investments and leadership to loosen these ties.

A promising step forward is that cities around the world—Aspen, San Francisco, Copenhagen, Bonaire, and Munich as of the writing of this book—are committing to transition to 100 percent renewable electricity by 2020 or 2025.[9] In 2016, Germany became the first country in the world to generate as much as 34 percent of its electric energy from renewables. But we need to see exponential levels of growth in the renewable energy sector, beyond current predictions, to make a serious dent in worldwide greenhouse emissions. Up until now, the public and private sectors have invested much more cautiously in the renewable energy sector, because the cycle of the technology to realize returns has historically been longer than investments in faster returning sectors, like digital or medical technology.

Climate change is clearly one of today's biggest innovative challenges. Fortunately, a small but growing group of leaders have fully engaged the issue, with some of them even listing fighting climate change as part of their mission.

Moving toward grid parity and better battery storage

Any real solution to the problem of greenhouse gas emissions will include rapidly growing the use of renewable energy. Achieving "grid parity"—in which the cost of renewable energy is equal to the cost of dirty, carbon-based energy—is a key to rapid adoption. This, in turn, relies on developing more effective and cheaper energy storage technology. Most renewable energy sources—solar and wind—are intermittent. With advanced battery systems, people could cheaply store the abundant power of the sun, steeply dropping the costs of solar-based electricity.

Tesla Motors, Panasonic, and SolarCity are partnering to develop lithium battery storage technology to make solar and wind power much more energy efficient. Many other companies, like ABB, Primus Power, and Samsung, are following suit. The battery technology to store solar power for residential and commercial use is available, but the demand will go up when the cost comes down over the next few years.

In a 2015 interview with *The Atlantic*, Microsoft founder and philanthropist Bill Gates urged on this imperative to invest much more in renewable energy technology to mitigate climate change: "I want to tilt the odds in our favor by driving innovation at an unnaturally high pace, or more than its current business-as-usual course."[10]

Licensing a lifestyle

Transforming the car industry, which is the second biggest contributor to green-house emissions, will go a long way toward combatting climate change. In this case, the transformation will not only be the result of new technology, but will also come from reimagining the way mobility is delivered.

Ana Arriola, Founder and CEO of Minimalisms, a premier product design con-sultancy, and previously an employee of Apple, Sony, Adobe, and Samsung, told me she already sees a huge change in how car companies imagine car ownership.

> Within the next five years you're going to see a lot more of an aggressive push from all of the big automotive manufacturers to move away from "buy an automobile" to "subscribe to our service," which is really "license a life-style." So, license an Audi lifestyle. License a BMW lifestyle. Then, if you do that, it's going to be easier and more effective to deliver a car that is always having the latest technology that is better for us and our planet without having to make a bunch of them and some of them might not sell.

In addition to demanding new ownership models, younger people are likely to not own cars at all. They are very comfortable with using Lyft and have a more favorable view of public transit than other age demographics. Perhaps these changes are also driven by their lower-paying jobs and higher rates of unemployment; the younger generation is more likely to see ownership of a car as cumbersome and wasteful. The adaption of fully autonomous vehicles, which some experts believe will begin in the next year or two, will only lessen the demand for ownership.[11] The combination of more efficient autonomous vehicles and lower ownership rates can reduce carbon emissions much more quickly than adaption of hybrid and electric vehicles alone.

All these solutions for reducing greenhouse gas emissions, from clean energy and transportation to battery storage technology, are already being developed by innovative future-leaning companies. Providing solutions to global warming is a huge growing business opportunity for future first companies that see the advantage of having a positive impact on the environment. As climate change becomes more real and apparent to consumers and business leaders, there will be unlimited opportunities to offer solutions that accelerate the evolution to low carbon ecosystems in energy, transportation, and agriculture.

Innovation challenge #2: resource scarcity

There is another way in which modern economies are running up against the realities of a finite world. Whether it is minerals, land, or other commodities, we are getting closer to exhausting the earth's capacity. In fact, we could run out of zinc, silver, gold, copper, and lead before the middle of the century.[12] The commercial importance of these raw materials has set off a scramble to buy up resources. For example, the Chinese government and private Chinese companies have spent billions of dollars buying up the mineral assets of African countries since the late 2000s. China needs these raw materials to continue manufacturing mountains of cell phones and toasters. To secure the approval of local governments, it frequently offers loans to these cash-starved countries. Over the past several years, China has actually loaned more money to the African continent than the World Bank.

An even more fundamental resource is also reaching peak capacity: clean drinking water. In 2015, the World Economic Forum reported that the global water crisis is the largest risk we face. Population growth and rising standards of living in developing countries mean that at least 9.8 billion people will need adequate water, food, and homes by 2050. According to this math, we would need to double the availability of fresh water by 2050.[13] On top of the rising demand to have more water for drinking and sanitation, the rising demand for food and homes also requires more fresh water.

In the future, wars may be fought specifically over water access, much the same way countries have battled for oil access over the past 100 years. Among the other reasons for the Syrian Civil War that claimed the lives of hundreds of thousands of people is the country's drought between 2007 and 2010, the worst in recorded history. Crops were destroyed, food prices rose, and 1.5 million out-of-work Syrian farmers moved from rural areas into cities.[14] This social unrest sowed the seeds for a brutal civil war. Scientists suggest that the Syrian refugee crisis is a terrible preview of what could become worse in the Middle East, the Mediterranean, and other places because of resource scarcity.

In addition to the disruptions to commercial activity, the private sector will also be enormously affected by a severe water shortage. More than 20 percent of the world's GDP today is produced in water-stressed regions. Agriculture alone uses 70 percent of today's fresh water withdrawal.[15] Water-intensive business industries, like agriculture and apparel, are now scrambling to find cost-effective solutions to the looming challenge of surging demand and already deficient supplies for clean and safe water sources.

Water processers, social messaging, and industry leadership

Over 2 billion people in the world don't have access to proper sanitation systems, which means their waste ends up in the water supply of millions of people, killing or sickening many of them in the process. The Omniprocessor, an innovative business funded by The Gates Foundation, is working on solutions to this global problem by burning human excrement safely at extremely high temperatures and producing clean drinking water from that waste. But instead of using tons of fuel, like most sewage plants around the world, the Omniprocessor powers itself with a steam engine and even produces excess electricity.

The next generation Omniprocessor, which is being piloted in Dakar, Senegal, has the capacity to handle waste from 100,000 people, and to produce 86,000 liters of potable water a day and a net 250 kilowatts of electricity.[16] Talk about closed loop production—from human waste to fresh water and renewable energy. The Omniprocessor will run on a system of sensors and webcams that allow the engineers to control the processor remotely and diagnose problems with the team in Dakar.

3D printing

General Electric and many other companies are now exploring the possibilities of another new technology with the potential to massively reduce waste in manufacturing. A 3D printer builds objects by adding multiple layers of a material until it produces a final unit. This doesn't sound revolutionary, until one realizes that most manufacturing does the opposite. Traditionally, production makes almost everything by taking a big raw material and cutting and hammering and molding and prying it until the final product emerges. But much of what is left over—the stuff that was cleared away—becomes waste on the production floor. With 3D printing there is no production floor. The results in terms of material and costs saved can be huge, up to 90 percent. Depending on the product, 3D manufacturing could also use around half as much water.

Though the technology exists, it will take another five to ten years for 3D printing to become cost-effective for businesses and consumers. "What you're going to see is that move from the lab prototype area to industrial capability," explained Ana Arriola. "You can actually deliver to the store, to the consumer hands, something that was literally printed for them or printed for that product. Then you're going to see that trickle down into the homes or into the neighborhoods." Companies from General Electric to UPS to SAP are investing heavily in the potential of 3D printing to remake manufacturing into a smarter and nearly zero waste model. These innovative solutions will accelerate the transition to lower resource usage across the ecosystems of food, clothing, consumer goods, and technology.

The zero discharge coalition

In 2011, Greenpeace published two "Dirty Laundry" reports[17] showing that factories supplying major fashion brands were discharging a range of hazardous chemicals into rivers in China, polluting waterways. The report also showed that clothing and certain fabric-based shoes sold by major fashion brands were manufactured using NPEs, highly toxic hormone-disrupting chemicals.

One of the companies implicated, Nike, formed an industry-wide coalition with Puma, Adidas, and H&M to commit to zero discharge of hazardous chemicals in their global supply chains by 2020. The Zero Discharge coalition has since been joined by sixteen other brands, including Gap, Levis, New Balance, Benetton, and Burberry. Then the chemical companies that worked with these manufacturers joined the pledge. Although the innovation did involve technological advances, equally important was how the companies approached the problem. They created an industry-wide alliance where the competing companies could collaborate around a major problem. The bigger innovation in this case was the positive ecosystem that developed around a specific problem. Once everyone is trying to eliminate the chemicals, innovative new solutions arise. These alliances are one of the most powerful ways that future first leaders can make rapid, industry-wide change a reality.

Nike's response, a meaningful commitment to eliminate a chemical on an established timeline, is also essential in an age of unprecedented social media transparency. If a global company or any of their suppliers are doing something irresponsible on the other side of the world, they will get called out eventually. And the news travels faster than ever. Greenpeace has a membership of 3 million people, an email list many times that size and the ability to get its items picked up by thousands of media outlets. And the negative PR impact is lasting. Even today, a Google search quickly reveals the original report from 2011.

But future first companies know how to invest in building their brand and reputation for solving global challenges. They recognize that not only are there guaranteed opportunities for future first companies, but also there are nearly guaranteed penalties for not being future first. Nike has gotten ahead of social media transparency by turning the pressure to be more responsible into an opportunity to lead industry changes.

Innovation challenge #3: social dynamism

All sorts of demographic data point toward a future full of social dynamism. As just one example, try to guess what the five largest cities in the world will be in twenty-five years. Hint: There is no Beijing, Shanghai, New York, or Mexico City on the list. Instead, countries in Africa and India will dominate, including Mumbai, Kolkata, Kinshasa, Delhi, and Dhaka. Between them, these cities will have close to 200 million inhabitants by 2050.[18] The massive changes in population growth, urban density, and socio-economic conditions will be just as big an innovation challenge as the looming lack of raw materials or climate chaos. And all three challenges reinforce each other in multiple ways, amplifying their impacts.

These changes will also have major impacts in many developed nations. For example, California is the United States' first non-white majority state. By 2050, the whole country will follow suit.

Gender roles also continue to become more egalitarian and less segmented by the historically separate domains of work and home, putting pressure on the workplace to adapt. In her book, *Marriage, a History: How Love Conquered Marriage*, family historian Stephanie Coontz notes that until the late 1970s, husbands—but not wives—were legally obligated to financially support their families, while wives were legally obliged to perform services in the home.[19] Today women represent 47 percent of the US workforce. In a year or two, women will be the majority of workers, and an increasing number of them will be the primary breadwinners.[20]

The traditional boundaries between the workplace and home life have become much more permeable (and sometimes almost non-existent), giving workers across many industries more flexibility to take care of family and home responsibilities. But the top leadership positions in most high-powered industries, like finance, technology, and business, still depend heavily on traditional gender roles. According to these traditional roles, the male breadwinner has a much greater capacity to put his time and attention into work (and travel for work as needed), because he has fewer day-to-day family responsibilities in the home. And the female homemaker or worker, who more often structures her career around her family's schedule, puts the responsibilities of her children, elders, and home first, taking a major hit in her earning potential over her lifetime as a result.

Yet the traditional gender roles that hold many high-powered careers in place at the top are running smack up against the social reality that non-traditional families are on the rise. Non-traditional families are those with two breadwinners, the wife as the primary breadwinner, single parents, parents cohabitating outside of marriage, and same-sex parents. The increased awareness of gay, lesbian, bi-sexual, and transgender identities flusters traditional ideas and norms about gender roles.

The number of multiracial families is also growing. In the US, the number of multiracial babies grew from 1 percent in 1970 to 10 percent in 2013, and their numbers will continue to rise.[21] These changes aren't just a matter of one group growing while another group shrinks. Biracial identities tend to blur the whole idea of race.

To be effective at hiring and managing people, business leaders will need to understand these rapid and irreversible social changes. Many powerful industries, like finance and technology, are starting to examine why the next generation of more diverse talent isn't getting hired or promoted at anywhere near the same rate that they are graduating from college or entering the workforce. And leaders across many industries will have to respond much more inclusively than they have responded to date.

Failing with white male boards

Starting in the 1960s, some American businesses did begin to make efforts to diversify their boards of directors. With very few exceptions, the leadership of the nation's top companies was all white men. The civil rights movement nudged them to make their membership more representative of the country's population. They failed. Today, white men make up about 31 percent of the US population, but they make up nearly 70 percent of the boards of directors of Fortune 500 companies. White women, about 32 percent of the total population, make up fewer than 17 percent of these directors. The total percentage of non-white directors at the top 500 companies is even less representative. Despite being over 37 percent of the US population, non-whites make up only about 14 percent of directors at Fortune 500 companies.[22]

Businesses cannot continue to fall so short of these goals. In the past, it was a disappointment. In the future, it will be fatal. Today, companies with black and brown faces on their teams crow about their diversity. In decades to come, the vast majority of the total workforce will be non-white. By selecting from this larger talent pool, companies that excel at empowering diverse talent will have an overwhelming competitive advantage.

But it goes further than this. Diversifying the leadership of a company to better reflect the population of the US is only a first step for companies with global ambitions. The overwhelming majority of global population growth will be in Asia, Africa, and Latin America. By 2050, people of European ancestry will be only about 10 percent of the world's population. You can't realistically hope to understand, much less compete, in the future with a board full of white men.

Artificial intelligence (AI) and the Internet-of-Things

Adapting leadership skills to a more diverse, less hierarchical world is easier for some people than others. It also only helps with humans. We have become accustomed to software and machines automating many jobs, from stock market trades to the assembly of a Tesla Model S. But AI software is taking the participation of non-sentient beings to the next level. AI will increasingly be processing big data. It will not make decisions, but it can generate algorithms to inform decision-making processes, like a medical diagnosis or a lending decision.

Gartner, a leading information technology and research company, estimates that by 2019 retail cloud computing will double in size to $314 billion, and the sensors on objects will increase 250 percent, to a $2.6 trillion business.[23] A few companies, like Google and Amazon, will be positioned to develop even greater monopolies of their markets through big data processing capabilities. Along with self-driving cars, software-based personal assistants, and service robots, humans will have a new relationship with computers.

Projects run by companies like General Electric and IBM are helping to create this new model by developing what they call the "Internet-of-Things," which refers to responsiveness between people and things. Such responsiveness is created by having devices and sensors on everything from streets to car bumpers to hydroelectric dams that wirelessly connect to faraway data centers, where millions of computer servers manage and learn from all that data. Servers send back commands to help systems to operate more effectively. In this way, big data processing will enable rapid and automated adjustments to systems like home heating and streetlights, as well as insurance decisions after a car accident.

Varthana creates a new education ecosystem in India

In India, as in many other developing countries, there is a massive baby boom underway. Today, there are more than 400 million school-age children in India, and only two-thirds of them attend school. This is despite the fact that Indian parents of all income levels view education as the key to their children's future. Even low-income Indian families will sacrifice as much as 13 percent of their income on affordable private school so their kids don't have to go to the government schools, whose quality is known to be very poor.[24]

Because of this demand for education in India, more than 200,000 small grassroots private schools have sprung up around the country, and they need capital and capacity. Two social entrepreneurs, Steve Hardgrave and Brajesh Mishra, saw that India's future will be shaped by how quickly school-age children get access to high-quality affordable private education. They started a company called Varthana, headquartered in Bangalore, which provides small loans to affordable private schools and partners with the school owners to build their capacity.

In an interview for this book, co-founder of Varthana, Steve Hardgrave, vividly described the global challenge that he built his company to address. Steve said:

> You are talking about a 430 million student-age population in India right now and this is a situation . . . which has never ever occurred and will never occur again in the history of the world. India is at that baby boomer stage. And so much of the India population is living at or around the poverty line. And the government budget and system for education is entirely overwhelmed, and so the vast majority of these young people with low resources are getting a very poor quality education.

Varthana is responding to the huge demand for solutions to transform the ecosystem of education in low- and middle-income countries with a swelling population. The hope is that other promising companies will follow their lead.

Future first business leaders who truly understand the social dynamics of changing demographics around the world will be way ahead on the talent game. The laggards who hang on to the old power structure will lose their effectiveness as leaders, and their ability to hire, develop, and retain the best talent will wane. There will continue to be gaps between the demographics of who is in charge and those who are up and coming in the workplace. But open-minded leaders who can listen to their employees and learn from them will be better able to adapt their companies to the challenge of social dynamism.

The urgency of tomorrow

As innovation challenges increase over the next few years, more Fortune 500 business leaders will truly understand and get excited about addressing them. They will better understand the enormous impact that their companies are having on our global societies and our environment. At the same time, smaller innovators will scale their best solutions and business practices. When they do, future first leaders will focus less on business-as-usual strategies and short-term business results and more on investing in accelerating innovation to push their value frontiers.

I frequently hear from business leaders who are highly motivated to do everything they can to solve complex global problems. They often have a sense of urgency, and want the world to move faster to achieve the scale and speed of change they know is needed to address global problems like climate change, resource scarcity, and social dynamism. But while these big innovation challenges are relatively well-known, there are opportunities in nearly every industry. The most important solutions will not come from those waiting for regulations and exposure to risks and disasters to force them to change. The solutions will come from the innovators who get out ahead of these future challenges.

Notes

1 Cendrowski, S. (2016, December 19). Massive smog blanket prompts pollution red alert in Beijing. *Fortune*. Retrieved from http://fortune.com/2016/12/19/smog-red-alert-beijing-china/
2 England, C. (2016, November 23). Climate change happening 'too fast' for plant and animal species to adapt. *The Independent*. Retrieved from www.independent.co.uk/news/science/climate-change-extinction-species-happening-too-fast-for-plant-and-animals-to-adapt-a7433111.html
3 Howard, B. (2016, June 14). First mammal species goes extinct due to climate change. *National Geographic*. Retrieved from https://news.nationalgeographic.com/2016/06/first-mammal-extinct-climate-change-bramble-cay-melomys/
4 Kolbert, E. (2015). *The sixth extinction: An unnatural history*. New York, NY: Henry Holt & Company.
5 Intergovernmental Panel on Climate Change (IPCC). (2015). Climate change 2014: Synthesis report. www.ipcc.org Retrieved from www.ipcc.ch/report/ar5/syr/

6 Hoff, M. (2013, April 19). Steve Howard: Ikea-style sustainability. *Ensia.* Retrieved from http://ensia.com/interviews/steve-howard-ikea-style-sustainability/

7 Ibid.

8 Scott, M. (2014, August) Coal to be hardest hit by fossil fuel divestment campaign. *Forbes.* Retrieved from http://www.forbes.com/sites/mikescott/2014/08/26/coal-to-be-hardest-hit-by-fossil-fuel-divestment-campaign/#52a74e79246b

9 Grover, S. (2015, January). 10 cities aiming for 100 percent clean energy. *Mother Nature.* Retrieved from http://www.mnn.com/earth-matters/energy/stories/10-cities-aiming-for-100-percent-clean-energy

10 Bennet, J. (2015, November). We need an energy miracle. *The Atlantic.*

11 Heath, C. (2015, December 12). How Elon Musk plans on reinventing the world (and Mars). *GQ.*

12 Desjardins, J. (2014, September 4). A forecast of when we'll run out of each metal. *Visual Capitalist.* Retrieved from http://www.visualcapitalist.com/forecast-when-well-run-out-of-each-metal/

13 Multiple ways of assessing threats to water: Supply-side and demand-side problems. (2017, September 22). Retrieved from http://www.fewresources.org/water-scarcity-issues-were-running-out-of-water.html

14 Sample, I. (2015, March) Global warming contributed to Syria's 2011 uprising, scientists claim. *The Guardian.*Retrieved from https://www.theguardian.com/world/2015/mar/02/global-warming-worsened-syria-drought-study

15 Khokhar, T. (2017, March 22). Chart: Globally, 70% of freshwater is used for agriculture. *The World Bank.* Retrieved from https://blogs.worldbank.org/opendata/chart-globally-70-freshwater-used-agriculture

16 Gates, B. (2015, January 5). This ingenious machine turns feces into drinking water. Retrieved from http://www.gatesnotes.com/Development/Omniprocessor-From-Poop-to-Potable

17 Greenpeace (2011, July 13). Dirty laundry: Unravelling the corporate connections to toxic water pollution in China. Retrieved from http://www.greenpeace.org/international/en/publications/reports/Dirty-Laundry/

18 Hoornweg, D. & Pope, K. (2014, January). Population predictions of the 101 largest cities in the 21st century. *Global Cities Institute,* Working Paper No. 4.

19 Coontz, S. (2006). *Marriage, a History: How Love Conquered Marriage.* New York: The Penguin Group.

20 US Department of Labor 2010 fact sheet. (2010). Retrieved from http://www.dol.gov/wb/factsheets/qf-laborforce-10.htm

21 Pew Research Center (2015, June 11). Multiracial in America. Retrieved from http://www.pewsocialtrends.org/2015/06/11/multiracial-in-america/

22 The Heidrick and Struggles Board Monitor. (2017). Board diversity at an impasse? Retrieved at http://www.heidrick.com/Knowledge-Center/Publication/Board-Monitor-2017

23 Hardy, Q. (2016, January 1). Looking beyond the Internet of Things. *The New York Times.*

24 Bajaj, V. and Yardley, J. (2011, December 30). Many of India's poor turn to private schools. *The New York Times.*

3   Selecting the future with big questions

From multinational corporations to small startups, companies from across many different ecosystems are adopting new business practices to meet innovation challenges. But they all start the same way: asking profound questions about the future of a particular industry or sector. The examples given in this chapter are in no way meant to be an exhaustive list of such questions. Instead, they provide insight into how successful leaders and companies have identified opportunities for innovation that could truly expand their value frontier.

Successful businesses are usually in markets saturated with competitors, where value comes from gaining better margins through higher prices and greater cost efficiencies. FedEx gains better margins by charging a little more than the competition while implementing cost efficiencies in their vast fleet of trucks and systems to monitor the speed of their deliveries. Once business leaders have exhausted their options for better margins, they seek new strategies for expanding their products and services into adjacent markets. Starbucks added meals to go, like hot breakfast sandwiches, to their original coffee menu. But leaders are usually cautious about reinventing their core business by going into entirely new markets, because it is considered riskier, both on the upside and the downside.

However, if you look at your business risks over a longer horizon, like five to ten years out, you will see that big intractable challenges, like climate change, resource scarcity, and social dynamism are not going away. They are practically guaranteed to continue presenting mounting risks and opportunities for your business. Future first leaders can generate enormous value by getting out ahead of these challenges, rather than losing value by becoming laggards in their industry. They can manage real and certain risks to their business, and be prepared to invent or reinvent their core business, rather than being caught by surprise. Future first leaders are constantly future-proofing their business by asking big questions.

What is the future of investing?

The first chapter introduced a huge challenge in traditional business accounting. By labeling side effects of commercial activity like pollution or income inequality, this accounting magically disappears them from the spreadsheet. Over the past several decades, a growing number of investors have innovated new ways to include these externalities in their bottom line. Once these challenges are identified and assigned a value, companies are encouraged to pursue novel efforts to mitigate or correct them.

Nancy Pfund and double bottom line investing

In 2001 tech investment bank Hambrecht and Quist's (H&Q) CEO, Dan Case, asked managing director Nancy Pfund to move from overseeing venture capital to managing the company's philanthropy, and then to developing a community development VC fund at H&Q, which was designed to invest in the local community as a way to create new companies and develop more local jobs. At the time, community groups in the region were disappointed that Silicon Valley growth didn't give jobs to the lower income neighborhoods of the local community. "We looked at job creation, place, sustainability, quality of jobs, community engagement," said Pfund. "We developed several metrics and also worked with the Ford Foundation on crafting a formal approach." With one foot in philanthropy and the other firmly in the day-to-day for-profit venture activities, Pfund became an early creator of a new investment strategy.

Philanthropy itself was nothing new. But, often, it remained divided from business practices. Probably the best known example of this contradiction is John D. Rockefeller. The oil baron gave generously throughout his life, notably to African-American Baptist churches and schools; Spelman—the nation's premier historically African-American female college—is named after Rockefeller's wife, Laura Spelman Rockefeller. The same man became the wealthiest man in recent history through cutthroat business practices, including crushing competitors and strike busting that, among other incidents, resulted in what became known as the "Ludlow Massacre." While laws have been created and norms have changed to reduce the severity of these kinds of practices, many corporations today still maintain a firm separation between philanthropy and business practices.

Pfund asked if it was possible to break down the firewall between the two. The result was an early version of what became known as "double bottom line" investing. She established a fund that accounted for both traditional bottom line profit as well as metrics relating to social and environmental impact.

In the late 1990s, H&Q went through a series of acquisitions and mergers with large financial institutions. Partly as a result of these changes, Pfund created the $75 million Bay Area Equity Fund (BAEF) in 2004, eventually spinning it off from JPMorgan. In 2008, she formed DBL Investors—Double Bottom Line—taking the BAEF with her. Her next fund, DBL Equity Fund, was $150 million, and her most recent one, DBL Partners III, is $400 million.

Pfund has been successfully prototyping social impact investing since before it had a name. Like all venture capitalists, she is still looking for companies with the potential to deliver top tier market rate returns. At the center of Pfund's investment philosophy is also the company's potential social impact. "We're always in the back of our mind thinking, 'What would be the impact? What are the ways we could create impact with this company?'" said Pfund.

DBL has two definitions of social impact. The most obvious are business models with impact baked in. For example, SolarCity (acquired by Tesla in 2016) could only achieve growth if it expanded the usage of renewable energy—a material net gain for the environment. The company also created thousands of accessible solar installer jobs. A second business model has a social impact that is less obvious. These are companies in which the primary commercial activity does not necessarily create social benefits that are readily apparent. At the same time, the management team is committed to creating double bottom line—not just as traditional philanthropy, but as a way to build competitive advantage.

Streaming music site Pandora, for example, might not appear to be innovating around any social challenges by providing music via the internet. However, the company's active engagement with local Oakland neighborhoods is part of a strategy to attract talent and build positive community relationships. Pandora's engagement is important because it points the way for companies from virtually any sector to use double bottom line accounting. Demonstrating that any company can have double bottom line impact is, in fact, part of DBL Partners' mission. "We really do want to show the world that there are great impact companies that are obvious, but then don't let any companies off the hook for being capable of designing significant impact, even if it is not as obvious," said Pfund.

What is the future of social responsibility?

Over the past ten to fifteen years, the internet has flooded us with information about social challenges. We can now easily access enormous amounts of data and research about living conditions in India or ocean acidification's impact on oyster farms. This situation alone has compelled a new crop of social innovation companies to ask how they can be socially responsible as a baseline before innovating into business models. Typically, these companies provide solutions to big social problems driven by enormous power inequities around the world, like access to healthy affordable food, clean water and sanitation, electricity, and affordable quality education. One advantage these companies enjoy is that the same internet-enabled awareness of the social problems can also prime consumers and investors to get excited about a new solution.

Revolution in the school cafeteria

Kirsten Tobey met Kristin Groos at Haas Business School. Tobey had a background in education and the non-profit world, while Groos had started in investment banking, and the two found a common cause in creating a business that could create a positive impact in education. The result is Revolution Foods, a company that aims to replace less-than-healthy and unappetizing school lunches with healthier, tastier meals.

Tobey and Groos graduated from Haas Business School in 2005 without traditional jobs at investment banks or consulting firms. Instead they had an innovative business plan. By 2005, public awareness about an obesity epidemic in the United States was widespread. One in four American children was obese and one in three children from low-income families was obese. This extra weight was putting kids at much greater risk for diseases like diabetes and heart disease. Revolution Foods committed to solving this big, well-defined social problem with a business solution first. Tobey recalled an early source of inspiration:

> I remember this one moment when we were first starting out. We sat down with a principal of a charter school, and we were trying to figure out if she would consider working with us. And I remember her saying, "please, please don't let this just be a business school project. The world needs better food for our kids in schools like ours." And so we began being pulled by this much greater social need, because there is nobody else out there doing this.

Then they came up with an innovative solution: partnering with urban schools to provide healthy affordable kid-friendly meals that were also eligible to receive funding through the federal school meals program. Soon after graduation, they received their first round of venture capitalist funding from Nancy Pfund at DBL Partners, then leading JPMorgan's BAEF. Since they launched Revolution Foods in 2007, the company has expanded from its beginnings in Oakland to hundreds of schools across the country to the East Coast. They've also launched a branded line for grocery stores, making healthy options easy for parents.

Another player in the mission to bring healthy food to school cafeterias is Red Rabbit, headquartered in New York City. Founded by Rhys Powell, Red Rabbit aims to grow and scale into an inspiring example of how healthy food can be done in schools. Powell told me in an interview:

> Our primary impact on our community is changing the way or improving the way that the 13,000 kids who eat our food every day see food. And by exposing them to quality made-from-scratch meals every day, we're impacting how they, and hopefully their families, interact with food. They are then able to make good choices.

What is the future of consumption?

For as far back as most consumers can remember, there has been a general preference for the new. Gifts needed to be straight out of the packaging. Shoes were more exciting in the box, and cars seemed to drive better with that smell of volatile organic compounds. Longevity didn't matter. We bought cheap goods and replaced them often. In fact, even throwing away those goods, once used, was part of the consumption process. The result was an enormous amount of waste.

Among the large sources of this waste are electronics companies. Despite the companies' continual, rapid technological innovations, the environmental impact of their devices' components was not on their radar.

Ana Arriola, who has worked as a product designer and leader at Apple, Sony, Adobe, and Samsung, explained the old thinking about e-waste to me:

> When the first iPhone was coming out, there was nothing about global accountability and manufacturing change, or auditing of sustainable and eco-friendly materials. No one had really thought about going down to the motherboard level and thinking about where the components were sourced from, and what rare minerals they were derived from, or where were they manufactured and was there child labor involved?

This was true even when she worked on the more recent iPhone for the 2.5G and the 3G and the Apple TV initial installations. "No one in my group was talking about it," she said.

As awareness of these challenges has spread, companies like Apple and Sony have been forced to ask the question: How can we limit the negative environmental impact of consumption of our products? These questions have led to various types of innovation. They have begun to clean up consumption by starting with a cleaner product. Companies now demand access to sustainable materials, recycling, and ethical sourcing of the earth's minerals and rare motherboard components. Their commitment to, and interest in, sustainable product design is at the heart of these efforts, and the degree to which they can write down the cost of goods used at a large enough scale. Tech companies and their retailers have developed better and more accessible e-recycling programs. Best Buy has disposable yellow bins where you can dump your mobile phone for processing that includes taking out the batteries and separating all the components for resale, recycling, or reuse.

Beyond understanding where the components come from, some companies are innovating around the maintenance of their electronics. In product design today, a growing trend is for more electronics and technology companies to start thinking about how the consumer can easily take apart and remove the components of the board. Or, as Ana said, "if the assembly and construction of the screws can be easily accessed by a 'mere mortal,' then they do not have to be sent to a special support technical facility."

While they represent improvements in what we consume, none of these efforts deals with the central problem of consumption. By always seeking the new, we ultimately equate disposability with status and quality. The result was—and still is—an enormous amount of wasted things, wasted space, and wasted energy. But now some innovators are taking on this challenge.

Julie Wainwright and The RealReal

Nowhere is the hunger for newness more pronounced than in fashion. No matter how well a certain design sells, apparel companies must create a constantly revolving series of styles every season. For mass market consumption, the result is fast fashion: cheap, disposable product.

Enter Julie Wainwright, a veteran of the dot com era. Wainwright has been an executive at companies since the 1990s. At the tail end of the first tech boom, Wainwright was the CEO of Pets.com, which crashed out spectacularly. Undeterred, Wainwright continued to see value and growth in new ideas.

In 2011, during a conversation with a friend who would never shop on eBay or at any type of consignment store, Wainwright asked herself what a company would have to do to make selling used apparel, fine jewelry, watches, home goods, and art acceptable to consumers of high-end products. Her innovation, The RealReal, exists in a unique niche; it is a retail website that sells consignment luxury items and deals while emphasizing recycling and reusing.

The model for the business is relatively simple. Luxury managers for The RealReal go to private homes and evaluate lightly used high-end goods, from designer jackets to jewelry to furniture and art. The RealReal takes approved items, verifies their authenticity, prices them, puts them on their website, and ships them to buyers around the world. Wainwright said, "By adding authentication and inspection, by experts, we have added real value to the buyer." And the original owners get 60 to 70 percent of the resale value.

One of the big accelerators of The RealReal's success has been the partnerships they've cultivated with Neiman Marcus and Saks Fifth Avenue. These department stores introduced The RealReal to their big buyer base and endorsed them to consign. It's straightforward, but the site's success—it now has more than a million members—is a result of successfully replacing the value people often place on "new" with "real."

Recycling newspapers, glass, and plastic has, of course, been around for a long time. But there is no equivalent process for most of the apparel and accessories we pile up in our houses. Of her business model innovation, Julie Wainwright said:

> People have been buying used things for a long time. Our take is so different, because it is more palatable than buying it in an unregulated market. We treat items with integrity and respect. That is one of our key goals. We are part of changing people's perceptions. People change their patterns. They stop buying fast fashion and consume based on an item having value. Our whole concept was innovative.

Replicating The RealReal's model—displacing new purchases with desirable quality-assured used ones—could create a sea change in consumption patterns and the waste they generate. The RealReal has attracted several leading VC firms as investors, including DBL Partners, which specifically valued the social benefit of the circular economy nature of the company as well as its potential for strong returns.

Although it is in a completely different industry, The RealReal's model has more than a little bit in common with the sharing economy. In the case of Lyft and Uber, people have cars that aren't being used. Airbnb offers rooms that aren't being used. While the disruptive social impact of the Uber/Lyft and Airbnb business models have generated negative publicity on social media, especially in cities like San Francisco, the internet can help to monetize all this otherwise wasted capacity.

What is the future of money?

The story of the invention of the credit card goes like this. In 1949, a businessman named Frank McNamara got the bill for his dinner with an associate at New York's Major's Cabin Grill. McNamara realized he had forgotten his wallet and asked: "Why isn't there an alternative to cash?" McNamara and his partner, Ralph Schneider, started the first credit card—a small, cardboard card. Coined Diners Club, it spread quickly. By 1951, there were 20,000 Diner's Club cardholders, though it took another decade before the card was made from plastic.[1] Whatever the veracity of this origin story, it is irrefutable that consumers are continually transferring more and more of their transactions to non-material and electronic forms beyond what McNamara could have imagined.

Bitcoin, for example, can be used for infinitely small transactions with no transfer fee. Bitcoin's dispersed ledgers means it is decentralized and very secure. Square's small attachment allows small businesses to accept credit cards at a fee equal to or less than what traditional credit card companies charge. Instead of any expensive point of sale equipment, retailers just need a smart phone.

How PayPal and M-Pesa don't show you the money

Another financial innovator, PayPal, also makes it easier for small businesses, individuals, or anyone with an email address to send money electronically, either nationally or internationally, without going through the traditional banking system. PayPal started with the question: How could they innovate around the challenges faced by people who didn't use or have access to the full range of services offered by traditional banks?

The answer, according to VP of Global Consumer Products and General Manager, Consumer Financial Services and Venmo at PayPal, Joanna Lambert: "Transform financial services so that data can also help us to make transformative products that could change the future for some different constituents." Beneficiaries include young people who can't afford credit and are living paycheck to paycheck, and need to smooth out their cash flow.

These non-traditional financial services companies are also redefining the relationships with consumers, and between consumers and businesses, through the introduction of value-based limitations on how they will do business. For example, neither PayPal nor eBay allows consumers to use their sites to buy weapons. In April 2016, PayPal also announced they would stop plans to build a $3.6 million 400-person global operations center in Charlotte, North Carolina after the state instituted a "bathroom ban" that was considered discriminatory toward the LGBT community.[2]

Another financial innovation, M-Pesa, is targeted at consumers that are even further afield from traditional banking systems; it started out by allowing people in East Africa with no bank accounts to make payments using their cell phone. Cell phone ownership is common in East Africa, even among poorer people. M-Pesa allows small businesses to reduce risk by buying crop or livestock insurance. The demand for this service is huge. Roughly half of Kenya's financial transactions last year went through M-Pesa. By June 2016, 7 million M-Pesa accounts had been opened by Vodacom in Tanzania, and it has expanded into Afghanistan, South Africa, India, Romania, and Albania.

What is the future of energy?

To avoid climate disaster, we need to transform our energy usage from fossil fuels to renewables. The obvious responses to this challenge are being led by companies like SolarCity with their push to install renewable sources of energy. But this is only part of the future of energy. There is another aspect to this cleaner future, one often overlooked but every bit as important. Exploring this question begins by asking not just where and what will make our electricity, but how will we transport and store it? We can't charge and power our cell phones, computers, toasters, and cars without distributing this power. As of today, our means for doing this are limited, inconvenient, and, most importantly, wasteful.

Panasonic's billion-dollar gamble

Just as Toyota's CEO asked a fundamental question about the future of his industry, another huge Japanese company is asking: "What is the future of electricity?" Part of Panasonic's answer comes in the form of the $5 billion battery factory the technology company is partnering to build with Tesla. In some cases, we've seen leaders ask profound questions and respond with innovative but relatively small and inexpensive answers, like a hybrid business model or an elegant web platform. This is not one of those occasions. From its price tag to its physical size, nothing about the "gigafactory" is small. When completed, it will be the largest building in the world as measured in physical space, and entirely powered by renewable energy. Instead of agilely innovating around big challenges, Panasonic's partnership seeks massive economies of scale, which it will combine with new manufacturing processes.

One of the primary consumer products being manufactured in the gigafactory is not actually for powering cars, but is a home battery called the Powerwall. The Powerwall allows homeowners to store their renewable electricity from solar or wind over the course of the day. At night the Powerwall feeds electricity from solar power back into the house. The battery can also help smooth out the gaps in wind production. With cheap enough batteries, renewable energies would suddenly become as reliable and affordable as conventional grid power. Tesla's investment would also spur growth in, for example, solar array installing or wind turbine manufacturing.

The widespread adoption of cheap energy storage could also provide another answer to questions about the future of electricity. Today our power plants—coal, oil, solar, nuclear—need to produce the amount of electricity needed by customers at any given moment. If they overproduce, they have to get rid of the power somehow. They could, for example, simply convert the electricity to heat and let it burn off safely. One plant in the UK used to release excess electricity by heating a submerged metal plate. The power safely dissipated by warming the water in a lake. But the electricity was wasted.

The point is that there simply aren't many good ways to store electricity. Some power plants will use the extra juice to pump water uphill. In this way, the power is stored as potential hydroelectricity. During a usage spike, they can release the water back through a turbine. But an affordable, massive stack of batteries connected to the power plants would be a much more efficient and flexible storage system than dammed water. Instead of powering cameras, Panasonic's batteries could eliminate the surges and dips in power consumption. Electric waste would be reduced on a national scale. This would both make renewables more attractive and reduce the waste and carbon emissions caused by unnecessarily burning gas or coal.

Massive investment is exactly what battery technology desperately needs. Over the past several decades, many computing technologies receiving substantial private and public funding have grown dramatically. At the same time, funding for research in chemical science and battery technology has been relatively flat, leaving noticeable gaps in the development of electronics. Many wearable technologies still must be plugged in and charged regularly. But there is still not enough funding for innovation around the challenge of affordable battery technology that holds a charge for over a week.

But there is another, somewhat subtler dimension to this massive investment in battery technology: The designs will be open-source. In other words, anyone is allowed to use the battery technology in good faith. Innovators can use the technology as a jumping off point to ask a whole new set of questions about energy—spreading transformation across a whole ecosystem.

What is the future of apparel?

When we think of dirty industries, we tend to think of heavy manufacturing or chemical plants. But an unlikely culprit, apparel, is actually the second most polluting industry in the world. In terms of total toxicity, it is second only to oil—even though apparel is a much smaller industry in terms of revenue. The apparel industry uses enormous quantities of water for dyeing clothes and huge swathes of land for cotton production. Over the past few decades, big brand apparel companies have been forced to contend with labor abuses at their international suppliers' factories. Now, some are taking on these new sustainability challenges.

Cooking up sustainability in Nike's innovation kitchen

Nike, the most valuable sports brand and one of the top apparel companies in the world, asked itself how it could make a shoe that wasted less overall material.

The result was the flyknit shoe, a product that combines a proprietary high tensile strength thread called "flywire," which acts as a reinforcing element in the eyelets of shoes, with proprietary yarns that are made from 100 percent recycled PET bottles. The new technology weaves uppers with fewer pieces, resulting in up to an 80 percent reduction in material waste.[3] The enormous popularity of the flyknit shoe demonstrated to Nike and the world that they could successfully combine performance and sustainability.

Noah Murphy-Reinhertz is a designer at Nike, but he also reports to Hannah Jones, the VP of Sustainability. Just as social impact investor Nancy Pfund evaluates companies using the double bottom line of solid financials and potential social impact, Noah has to combine two considerations in sneaker product design. The core business of Nike is to enhance human performance through products. At the same time, the sustainability team is developing tools that they are attempting to get people to use across the whole company. Noah's question is: How can I bridge these two worlds of sustainability and innovative product design and creation?

Nike's "innovation kitchen"—the unit where designers can let their fervid imaginations go wild—has produced some answers to Noah's questions. One of Noah's responsibilities is communicating the needs of top athletes directly to the designers in the space kitchen. Shortly before I talked to him, Noah had met with long distance runner Galen Rupp.

> He's on his way down to the Olympics. He's coming off the Olympic trials, so we're asking him, "Okay, the shoe that we made for you, how does it feel? How does it perform?" We're also talking to his coach about where it's working.

In the early 2000s, the team at the innovation kitchen also came up with one of the most revolutionary redesigns of running shoes in the past few decades. Like many innovations, it began with designers going out and talking to coaches. Toby Hatfield heard about a study of Stanford athletes running on grass with no shoes. He took the idea back to Nike's facilities in Oregon and began running diagnostic tests on bare feet. Designers discovered that bare feet reacted totally differently than with padded running shoes on. It was a more natural stride, the way human feet had evolved for millennia. According to Noah, the innovation kitchen began "reimagining how could the shoe be more like a bare foot as opposed to this heavy duty thing that we put around our feet." The result was the Nike Free, a shoe with numbered levels of support, ranging from normal padded shoe (number 10) to nearly barefoot (1). The minimalist innovation has been a huge success for Nike.

As the company moves forward, they are creating a different kind of numbered scale: a footwear sustainability index. Each shoe will be scored on its environmental impact, with the scores becoming an important part of every development team's evaluation of the shoe as well as the shoe's annual review.

Women's fashion entrepreneur Eileen Fisher and her team are asking even bigger questions of the industry, like "What is the future of apparel? What should we be in the business of making for people to wear?" They set out a

2020 Vision to transform the company for long-term sustainability, by creating textile manufacturing processes that use less water and fewer toxic materials in fabric dyes. The company also uses mostly organic cotton in their products, further reducing the amount of pollutants in their products.

What is the future of everything?

Artificial intelligence, space elevators, life extension, archiving all the literature of the world—there is seemingly no limit to the projects that Alphabet, Google's parent company, will explore. Though virtually no one else has access to the sort of limitless financing that Alphabet provides its moonshot projects, this sort of unbounded questioning is how all leaders will find new challenges and new value frontiers to push.

But even Alphabet has additional criteria before they begin initial funding for innovation challenges. In their case: "Is this a billion-dollar industry? What are the future social and environmental impacts of the project?"

This combination of social and financial questions has resulted in funding a wide variety of experiments.[4] A Google contact lens measures the insulin levels of wearers through their tears. Another nanotechnology project with life-saving possibilities is a cancer-detecting pill. Alphabet's most famous undertaking, the self-driving car, could radically reduce the number of cars on the road while making them operate more efficiently and safely. The Loon Project imagines using weather balloons to float wireless routers, extending internet service to unwired parts of the world. Facebook followed suit by investigating the potential delivery of free wireless to people in developing countries using a series of connected planes that are extremely high up in the atmosphere.

Just as revealing are the projects Alphabet doesn't pursue. Some ideas are discontinued for practical reasons. The space elevator—a cheaper way to lift people and supplies into orbit—proved impossible until a stronger cable can be built. Early experiments with teleportation also fizzled out after researchers determined that the process violated the laws of physics.

Other queries were rejected for value-based reasons. The hoverboard was too costly relative to societal benefits; it wasn't going to suddenly encourage people to stop driving. The jetpack was rejected in part because it was too energy-intensive a form of transportation.

These moonshot projects can only be attempted by a huge corporation like Google or Facebook with the ability to finance research that has a high likelihood of never resulting in a useable product or service. But any leader can adopt the same openness to approaching innovation challenges that have a high risk of failure as well as a high upside, if solutions can be delivered. Once she or he finds an opportunity, there are more specific leadership mindset and organizational capabilities that can help deliver innovation. In the next chapter, we will delve into the future first leadership mindset that approaches global challenges as opportunities for innovating new forms of business value.

Notes

1 Diners Club. The story behind the card. Retrieved from https://www.dinersclubus.com/home/about/dinersclub/story.
2 Soper, S. and Green J. (2016, April 5). PayPal scraps plan to invest $3.6M in North Carolina after anti-LGBT law passes. *San Antonio Express-News*. Retreived from http://www.expressnews.com/business/national/article/PayPal-scraps-plan-to-invest-3-6M-in-North-7229551.php.
3 Nike. (2013, November 27). How Nike flyknit revolutionized the age-old craft of shoemaking. *The Guardian*. Retrieved from http://www.theguardian.com sustainable-business/partner-zone-nike1.
4 Karch, M. (2017, February 22) Google X, the secret Google Lab. *Lifewire*. Retrieved from https://www.lifewire.com/google-x-secret-lab-1616267.

4   Free your mindset

While I was researching and interviewing leaders for this book, I noticed that—for all their differences—they had some essential similarities. They held various positions in a variety of business models and in industries from cars to solar power. They were women and men, Swedish and Japanese, and identified with a variety of political and social views. But they all created environments where people are encouraged to innovate new business models, products, and services. What ultimately unified them, I realized, was a set of shared mentalities. As these mentalities became clearer, they reminded me of what the best-selling author and psychologist Carol Dweck calls "mindset." In a nutshell, mindset is the way in which people approach learning, failure, and success. Mindset is critical to how we learn to lead and how leaders help others learn to succeed in their jobs.

The seeds of Dweck's theory of mindset began early. When she was a sixth-grader in the 1950s, her teacher arranged the classroom seating chart according to students' "IQ score." Mrs. Wilson put the high-scoring students in the front of the room while lower scorers sat in the back. That sort of rigid assignment is unimaginable today; it had many of the anticipated negative impacts. Defined by a bad number, lower-scoring students were discouraged from learning and semi-segregated from academic activities. Their teacher even excluded them from non-academic privileges like carrying the flag or washing the blackboard.[1] The system taught hopelessness to the students who most needed to improve.

What was more surprising was how this arrangement affected the high-scoring students. One might assume that, treated like celebrities, high scorers would be incentivized to greater achievements. Instead, it made them paranoid. A poor grade on a test could prompt Mrs. Wilson to lower what she considered a student's "IQ." Dweck was a strong student, but she was terrified of exams. If she stumbled, Dweck knew she would lose her seat. Instead of being driven and engaged to learn, the fear of academic failure and demotion hovered over her all year.

Failing: to succeed

Dweck incorporated this experience into her later research as a psychologist and professor. In her 2006 book, *Mindset: The New Psychology of Success*, Dweck argued that our ability to learn is largely a matter of perception. Not only are many tests bad at capturing information about intelligence and capabilities, they actually discourage learning and future accomplishments. For Dweck, simply *believing* intelligence is fixed and quantifiable has a detrimental impact on humans' ability to learn.

This is largely because people who view IQ as an absolute, static number have little incentive to expand their learning. In Dweck's sixth grade class, "low IQ" students were led to believe they would never amount to much academically, no matter how hard they worked. Meanwhile, top ranked students were encouraged to keep doing what had made them successful: obsess over their performance on the next exam.

There was a second negative result of believing that accomplishments are tied to a fixed IQ. Trying to solve novel challenges—doing something no one has done before—increases the risk of failure. In an environment like Mrs. Wilson's class, would-be innovators were also taught to view any such failure as a humiliating downgrade of their overall intelligence. If a failure reflects a fundamental quality of unsuccessful experimenters, those students will be even more risk adverse. Many students preferred to look smart by successfully accomplishing tasks they could already do instead of expanding their experiences or knowledge base. They had adopted a static mindset.

In contrast, people who believe that intelligence is something you can grow and improve are more likely to challenge themselves. They are less afraid of failure and more likely to approach challenges as opportunities for learning. This doesn't make them "smarter." But it does make them more likely to increase their abilities and skills over their lifetimes. These people have a growth mindset.

Dweck's conclusion—the way people *understand* intelligence is a much better indicator of future success than IQ scores—has changed hiring practices. Employees with growth mindsets have a higher upside. Their mindset distinguishes them from otherwise highly qualified candidates who shy away from new challenges. This makes them more valuable to the organization.

From a people practices perspective, there is another important aspect of Dweck's thinking. Mindsets are not static. During the course of a day, we may toggle back and forth between different mindsets. People who bring enthusiasm to challenges at work may approach other aspects of their lives differently. Since mindsets are not fixed, leaders can deliberately develop their and their employees' approach toward growth and problem solving.

The same is true on the organizational level. Companies often have their own distinct mindsets. Each business's leaders, investors, employees, and board of directors has a specific way of approaching decisions as a group. When we talk about a company's "culture of innovation" or "conservative thinking," we are really talking about an organizational mindset.

As I became aware of the growth mindset common among future first leaders, I began to break down its most important aspects into five defining elements. For one, people with a growth mindset don't see problems as static constraints, but as innovation opportunities. These leaders are also able to think outside of the present tense, developing business models and products that can push the value frontier of the future. Although many of these leaders bring an element of idealism to their work, they are too pragmatic to be rigid idealists. Instead, they use flexible, integrative thinking to create profitable and scalable solutions to the world's biggest problems. Another unique element is that they expand on traditional "bottom line" decision-making processes to reveal all their value-based elements. Finally, these leaders often understand that real change is driven as much by cooperation between businesses and across ecosystems as by the heroic leadership of a single company.

I began to describe the mindset that this group of leaders shared as "future first." It was a growth mindset, but one with an emphasis on developing business innovations to meet pervasive social and environmental challenges: global challenges that are here to stay, and are even on the rise.

Embracing innovation challenges

A growth mindset does not shy away from problems, but is instead excited to solve them through ingenuity and creativity. Embracing global challenges as opportunities for innovation, rather than denying and ignoring them, is the most critical element of a future first mindset. It is how Eiji Toyoda asked the question, "What is the future of automobiles?" that led to the invention of the Prius. Every future first leader who is on the frontier of their industry has a mindset that is motivated by innovation challenges to remake their products and services for a more sustainable future.

Other aspects of the mindset that embraces innovation challenges are the attitudes and beliefs that drive a leader to dream of a different future, while maintaining a firm footing in the material reality of more and more billions of people using finite resources on a planet that can only handle so much waste and pollution. Embracing innovation challenges is a mindset element driven by relentless pragmatism and ingenuity.

Sony takes up the challenge of innovation

Jeanna Kimbré lives in Tokyo and heads up Studio Five, one of Sony's design studios, as well as Studio Nordic in Europe. Since she has been in Tokyo, Jeanna Kimbré has learned that Sony was, in a sense, born with mission-driven goals. The company started in 1946—the same year Japanese women got suffrage— in the devastating aftermath of World War II. Kimbré said that two elements of the company's DNA developed then. The first was the social responsibility of getting people into work. The other was engineering "the new and the next."

Today, the company pursues innovation in part through in-house competitions in which employees are encouraged to chase down an idea. Employees are invited into a "dragon den" full of high-ranking Sony officials. They pitch their idea. If it's good, they are encouraged to pursue it. Employees can take time off their normal jobs to follow up on their ideas. The idea isn't necessarily to create the next Walkman or PlayStation. In many cases Sony executives may realize, in Jeanna's words, that "if it is a good idea, it is inherently valuable." Today, Sony is a company of 128,400 employees around the world. They encourage individual employee effort as a way of what Jeanna describes as "not losing the small company mindset and the innovation part of that mindset."

Going solar is all about the financing

An early innovator in turning solar power into a multi-billion-dollar industry, Jigar Shah founded SunEdison in 2003. Shah described to me how he came up with the big idea of financing residential and commercial solar energy through the power purchase agreement business model. In his words:

> It basically dawned on me that people are used to working with their electric utility company, where you pay a connection fee and suddenly you have electricity. You don't pay for your slice of the coal plant that's feeding you. I thought that the solution to that would be to allow people to buy solar power as opposed to solar projects. Using their electricity bills to support financing, and it was really surprising to me, but it resonated really fast on the customer side. The investors took longer to bring on board but the customers embraced the model immediately.

Despite the fact that SunEdison filed for bankruptcy in 2016 because of mistakes made by its latest executives, the company had grown since its inception into the largest renewable energy firm, catalyzing the growth of the sustainable energy ecosystem. Since founding SunEdison, Shah has become a vocal clean energy leader on how companies can embrace new business models to mitigate climate change. He is the co-founder and President of Generate Capital and the author of *Creating Climate Wealth: Unlocking the Impact Economy*. He is the co-host of The Energy Gang, a podcast that explores technology, politics, and market forces driving energy and environmental issues. Shah exemplifies how future first entrepreneurs can embrace innovation challenges by creating commercially successful business models that create value within given environmental and social limitations—or that go even further and create value by reducing some of those limitations.

Overcoming presentism

Most of us are wired for the present. This can be helpful when we need to be totally focused on an immediate task, but it becomes a real impediment when we try to make decisions about the future. Given our reluctance to do things as simple as buying life insurance or sticking to a diet, it's really no surprise that we have trouble acting in the face of huge, de-personalized challenges like climate change. To many people, climate change seems distant, ominous, and unstoppable, like our mortality. We often deal with it in the same way: pushing the issue off into the distant future.

However, not everybody reacts the same way. Surprisingly, the biggest single factor between those who take action to combat climate change—or other global challenges—isn't simply their level of environmental commitment, but their mindset. Confronted with overwhelming data about the damage the global phenomenon is having and will have on the future of our planet, people with static mindsets prefer to ignore the issue and stick to what they know how to do. Faced with the exact same information, people with a future first growth mindset look for solutions. They are able to overcome their presentism.

This tendency toward ignoring future challenges goes well beyond the environment. Many companies are hobbled in adopting future-leaning business practices and products by their focus on short-term profits and goals. This inability to look years, much less decades, into the future results in lost opportunities to push their company's value frontier.

InVenture's credit rating app

Today it is incredibly hard for billions of people to borrow money. Although many of them will reliably pay back loans, with no financial profile, they have no chance to receive them from banks. This means that a huge chunk of the world's population is cut off from the most efficient ways of saving against disasters or investing in their businesses.

InVenture CEO Shivani Siroya knows how the current credit system works—and doesn't— her time at UBS and Citigroup. Entry into the traditional credit market is almost completely reliant on people's past financial history and current financial profile.

InVenture has an approach that is both novel and, once you hear about it, seemingly inevitable. Credit is essentially information. But decades into an information revolution, the way we measure credit has not changed dramatically from the mid-twentieth century. Though roughly a third of the world's population has no financial record, there are a billion smart phone users in the developing world. InVenture created an Android app that brings credit scoring into the future. Once borrowers download the app, it tracks over 1,000 data points—from texting friends to getting directions—that don't appear on traditional credit reports. "Over time this data is getting captured on these phones and it provides a really rich picture of a person's life," said Siroya.[2]

To demonstrate how the new credit model works, Siroya tells the story of a shopkeeper in Nairobi. The shopkeeper makes just enough to get by, but has no savings for a medical emergency or to expand her business. Before InVenture, her borrowing options were micro loans, which are extremely small, and loan sharks who charge up to 300 percent interest. She couldn't get a traditional loan. But after her son convinced her to download the InVenture app, it began tracking her normal smart phone activity in the form of a non-traditional credit score.

For example, the shopkeeper called her family in Uganda regularly. This improved her score by 4 percent because people who stay in touch with a few key contacts are better borrowers. From GPS, they could tell that she traveled a lot, but in consistent patterns. Location consistency was worth another 6 percent increase on her InVenture credit score. She also communicated with a large number of people. InVenture's research shows that network diversity is valuable; people who communicate with more than fifty-eight contacts tend to be good borrowers.

Once InVenture had collected all the data points, they decided to make a loan to the shopkeeper. Since then, she has not only successfully repaid her loan but has also used the money to expand her business to multiple locations. InVenture's ability to innovate beyond the presentism that is usually inherent in loaning money allows them to promote small entrepreneurial activity in the developing world. It also opens up a potentially enormous market for their new credit model.

Superforecasters beat the market

Ultimately, the 2008 financial meltdown was the result of widespread, collective, and devastating forecasting failures. Flush with profits, the financial industry ignored the risks of the mortgage-backed securities market. Regulatory agencies ignored signs of its impending implosion. Brokers encouraged low-income consumers to go on a credit binge. These consumers took on more personal debt—often with teaser entry rates—than they could afford over time. Everyone was sucked into what they could gain in the next few weeks or months. This overwhelming presentism nearly dragged us into the first depression in eight decades.

But not everybody missed the early warning signs. Michael Burry, the founder of hedge fund Scion Capital, LLC, saw the 2008 financial crisis coming several years ahead of most people and invested over a billion dollars in shorting the mortgage-backed securities market.

But the odds are that most readers think less like Burry and more like the mortgage-backed securities traders and the people who lost their houses. In their book, *Superforecasting: The Art of Science and Prediction*, Philip E. Tetlock and Dan Gardner demonstrate, based on their extensive research on forecasts made by tens of thousands of ordinary people, how only a handful of people are exceptional at accurately forecasting the future. Everyone else, they've found, is pretty bad at it. However, superforecasters do share a variety of cognitive skills that can be learned.

For example, they are less ideologically or professionally biased. They seek data from a wide range of sources to examine future trends. In Burry's case, he came from outside the financial industry and was a self-taught trader. Starting in 2004, Burry paid $100 a year to 10KWizard.com to gain access to the prospectuses of the mortgage bonds. He read the fine print that no one but the lawyers who wrote them actually read. He did the credit analysis that no one bothered to do to find the worst home loans that were getting bundled into the mortgage bonds. He put together a dozen factors that the banks weren't using to determine how likely those home loans would be to go bad.

Like Carol Dweck's growth mindset that enables learning, superforecasters are open-minded to all available information and analytic tools rather than shut down by ideological biases, limited data, or fear of making mistakes. Superforecasters also engage in probabilistic thinking, or understanding how statistical probability works, and they're more precise than the rest of us about assigning (and reassigning) probability levels to their hunches. Rather than starting with grand theories about the future of the economy or society—essentially cognitive biases—they assign probability levels to specific hunches or hypotheses that are not ambiguous. Burry brought a strong quantitative background to analyzing the probability of his initial hunch that the subprime mortgage markets would crash, and he used multiple sources of data to refine his forecasts. After doing his due diligence, the probability levels were high enough that he took some very big bets. That approach to the market drove him to develop different tools from other investors who were caught up in the daily rise in stock prices. With those tools he overcame the presentism that was dogging the rest of the financial and real estate markets.

It's impossible to lead in innovating and future-proofing your company if you can't get your head out of the now. Leaders with a future first mindset have a keen eye on future trends in technology, energy, and demographics. They seek and make sense of data, and track these trends with the goal of solving some of the biggest global challenges, like climate change, resource scarcity, and social dynamism.

Adopting integrative thinking

Enormous multinational corporations have contributed substantially to many of the global challenges we face today, from income inequality to resource scarcity and climate change. However, the knee-jerk tendency to reduce the world to greedy corporations vs. "do gooder" non-profits is a trap. Though their efforts are nowhere near sufficient today, more and more global corporations are taking big steps to solve global challenges. And, despite the outsized positive impact of social impact companies, most lack the size to innovate at the scale needed to address the biggest global challenges today.

Impact investing is one attempt to break down some of the traditional polarization between non-profits and socially driven companies and large multinationals. A pioneering leader of the impact investing movement, Jed Emerson, who founded www.BlendedValue.org, works with families on their impact investing strategies. Emerson told me, "It is overly simplistic to perpetuate the traditional notions of the evil capitalist and the righteous social worker." It is also counterproductive.

Coined by Harvard Business School Professor, Roger Martin, integrative thinking is the ability to bring together two seemingly contradictory ideas and to create something new.[3] Future first leaders bring this kind of flexible thinking to their organizations. They are purpose-driven and embrace new values while innovating around global problems. But they don't view traditional business models as fundamentally bad. They don't have an either/or approach to success.

Pipeline Angels

Natalia Oberti Noguera, who was on selected by *Inc. Magazine* as one of "The Most Impressive Women Entrepreneurs of 2016," is the founder and CEO of

Pipeline Angels. Pipeline Angels, a network of new and seasoned women investors, is changing the face of angel investing and creating capital for women and non-binary femme social entrepreneurs. In an interview, Natalia spoke with me on the importance of making space for the ambiguity between "doing good" and "doing well." As a cis LGBTQ Latina (she's half Colombian and half Italian), Natalia said, "I have been comfortable with hybrid models right from the start."

On solving Silicon Valley's problem of majority white employees in big technology companies, Oberti Noguera points out that marginalized groups must be represented in boardrooms. She is known to say, "If you want to be inclusive, be explicit."

White men in power can become allies by listening to marginalized voices, engaging in constructive dialogue on diversity that goes beyond placating underrepresented groups, and sponsoring (not just mentoring) more voices. Oberti Noguera referred to a study by the Annual Meeting of the Academy of Management that found that women, as well as men of color, are penalized for fostering diversity, whereas white men are viewed more positively (in terms of warmth and performance) when they do so.[4]

Building an integrative mindset across your board

Method Products was co-founded by Adam Lowry and Eric Ryan, who came from different but complementary professional backgrounds. Lowry, trained as a climate scientist, described their partnership as "high design and big sustainability coming together." While they have similar philosophies of leadership, their leadership styles are quite different.

Lowry initially thought it was important to have different areas of expertise represented on the board, but he believed everyone must have a fundamental willingness to listen. Method's board used to have "a more purely financial perspective" from the investor representation, and this wasn't ideal. Lowry realized they needed to have financial, social, and environmental perspectives included on the board as well. However, he knew the board also wouldn't work if it were atomized into different interest groups. "It's best if each person understands all of those outcomes, rather than we have the financial person, the environmental person, the social person. That doesn't work as well."

This was the situation at Method before it merged with Ecover in 2012, and both were bought by SC Johnson in 2017. When Ecover bought Method, the composition of the board completely changed. Now the merged board is made up of people who all have an integrative mindset and can weigh in on all kinds of business decisions. Looking back, Lowry reflected that it works much better to have the entire board made up of integrative thinkers.

A future first mindset requires integrative thinking to create profitable and scalable solutions to the world's biggest problems. Integrative thinking starts with synthesizing two seemingly contradictory ideas[5]—like making money and having a positive material impact—through innovative products, production practices, people practices, and partnerships.

Expanding values in business decisions

Value in the corporate world tends to be measured in terms that sound rational: profitability, competitive advantage, and productivity. But there is a lot that goes into business decisions that is left out of official work meetings. Any decision made by humans will be marked by emotions, personal attitudes, and other input that rarely is explicitly explored by the decision-makers themselves. These harder-to-measure inputs are critical to sound business decisions, because they represent the values of employees, customers, and shareholders.

The existence of these unexplored elements in decisions isn't a bad thing in itself. What's more, it's impossible to remove values from decision-making. Instead, we need to work toward developing effective tools and language to express and measure the breadth of values that are inherent in every business decision. We need to give human emotions and personal attitudes a seat at the table. This inclusion doesn't need to come at the cost of traditional "rational" criteria. Instead, leaders who have a broader understanding of their values can have a wider-ranging conversation about the true value of their companies to consumers, employees, shareholders, and many other stakeholders. In fact, some of the most irrational business decisions are often made when purely financial metrics eclipse human values.

When neurosurgeon Paul Kalanithi was dying of lung cancer at age thirty-seven, he began to assess the world around him differently. Like many terminally ill patients, he became more acutely aware of what he valued most. In his memoir, *When Breath Becomes Air*, he observed:

> Science may provide the most useful way to organize empirical, reproducible data, but its power to do so is predicated on its inability to grasp the most central aspects of human life: hope, fear, love, hate, beauty, envy, honor, weakness, striving, suffering, virtue. Between these core passions and scientific theory, there will always be a gap. No system of thought can contain the fullness of human experience.[6]

Similarly, traditional systems of rational business analysis don't fully capture a company's true value.

The past catches up to DuPont

In 1993, scientists working at DuPont Chemical concluded that the PFOA (perfluorooctanoic acid) used in many of their products, like Teflon, caused birth defects, cancer, and death. The leadership had to make a decision. Should they protect the health of consumers and neighbors and replace PFOA with safer alternatives? Or should they continue to use PFOA because changing it would put $1 billion of annual profit at risk? They chose the latter.[7]

For the next twenty years, DuPont knowingly leaked PFOA at more than twenty times the minimum risk level into the water supply of over 100,000 people living near their plants in Ohio and West Virginia. They also exposed their employees to highly toxic levels of the PFOA for years. The company protected its profitable business for a couple of decades, but in 2017 DuPont paid $670.7 million to settle over 3,500 civil lawsuits from private citizens who were sick and dying from PFOA exposure. The Environmental Protection Agency had only begun seriously regulating PFOA in 2015. And the fallout for DuPont is mounting—a recent plaintiff was awarded $5.1 million dollars.[8]

Among other things, DuPont's decision was guided by loss aversion, the cognitive bias to choose to limit smaller losses today rather than seek equivalent or bigger gains tomorrow. DuPont's choice was the result of a static mindset that seeks to hold on to today's known profits and is risk averse about seeking innovative solutions for the future that could incur loss or gain. But the upshot is that thousands of people are dying from DuPont's known chemical exposure, and the value of these human lives was not accounted for in twenty years of business decisions not to replace PFOA with available but more expensive substitutes.

Sometimes what appears at the time to be a perfectly rational business decision, like the decision made by DuPont to keep using PFOA and avoid annual profit losses of $1 billion, is at its core an irrational decision. From a purely financial standpoint, the company has paid less for the thousands of human lives lost so far than the amount of annual profit they have preserved every year since 1993. Yet, the loss of human lives, business reputation, and responsible leadership will erode the company's value in unforeseeable ways for years to come. And if DuPont had replaced PFOA with the less toxic alternative chemical available in 1993, they might have found innovative ways to reduce the additional costs over time. But when a complex business decision is made on the basis of a single metric, like profitability in the short term, it blocks out a number of other valuable inputs. The results may appear more irrational in retrospect. It is not unlike the rats in traditional psychology experiments that become addicted to cocaine and press the same button over and over to get more cocaine. Instead of pressing the button to get the food they need, they eventually die of starvation.

The language of emotion at work

Encouraging more emotional language at work is on the critical path to developing a growth mindset that allows people to take risks and be open to failure, which is a prerequisite for innovation at work. But a fixed mindset that avoids the vulnerability often required to take risks and sometimes fail is also a business liability. Not only do certain emotions fuel innovation and risk-taking, but they provide important data about a broader framework of business values.

But talking about love and experiencing vulnerability at work are often considered to be out of place and unprofessional. As Andrew Hoffman, Holcim (US) Professor of Sustainable Enterprise at the University of Michigan's Ross School of Business, said:

> You can start to bring in language that's very uncomfortable in a market setting, like "love," "sacred," and "holy." These are words that we as

intellectuals in the modern age mock. But at the end of the day, those are the only things that bring people to really care about something.

Creating new business models and innovating around the challenges of the future aren't just a matter of having the right financial data points. It also requires leaders to constantly examine the omnipresent role of a broader set of values inherent in their business decisions. Leaders need high emotional and social intelligence to understand the values of their employees, customers, and investors. Future first leaders can translate their stakeholders' values into business decisions that ultimately generate long-term value for the company and protect them from the losses that can come from the single-minded pursuit of financial gains.

Going beyond one-company, one-leader at a time

Companies today—even small ones—are more complex systems than they were forty years ago. They operate in the midst of an increasingly globalized environment held together by a massive physical infrastructure and powerful—and sometimes conflicting—political and economic interests. Leaders have to understand their companies in the context of all these larger systems, including global challenges like climate change, resource scarcity, and social dynamism. One, perhaps surprising, result of all this complexity has been companies discovering the value of working together.

Collaborating with your frenemies

Ingersoll Rand's Scott Tew described the move toward more collaboration among companies, saying:

> Most of the companies you've talked to have the same difficulties that we do in saying, "We're not quite sure how to solve this fully." A lot of times people will get you 50% of the way. Or we can shave 20% off of the waste or of the resource used, but we can't get you all the way to zero. I think sometimes we all have to be a bit humbler and say, "We can't solve this on our own, so we'd love to have some help and if you have any ideas, please step forward."

Likewise, Unilever's VP of Sustainable Business and Communications, Jonathan Atwood, described a similar need for greater collaboration across companies to solve problems like the stalled recycling movement or working with farmers' networks to be sustainable and have the right levels of biodiversity. As Atwood said, "It's not about more bins, it is about systemic change creating a breakthrough in the infrastructure. And are we prepared to collaborate to get there?" The open sourcing of Tesla cars and batteries is a new way of thinking about competition, one that is not threatened by sharing information but rather seeks to grow the whole ecosystem. The largest global challenges are too complex to be solved one-company, one-leader at a time.

Innovation within the limits of both profitability and sustainability can create and foster positive ecosystems. If someone creates an electric vehicle and corners the tiny market for electric cars, shutting out all competition, he or she is smothering the possibility of an ecosystem maturing around electric vehicles. This ecosystem will have a bigger impact on GHG emissions, but it will also raise awareness of electric vehicles and grow the market, perhaps resulting in more opportunities for the original innovator.

Future first leaders understand how their company is made up of many interdependent parts. They see how it's interconnected with partners, competitors, and consumers within wider ecosystems. They work to embed a future first mindset in their company's systems. The next chapter will describe how we can do this by developing a future first mindset and decision-making among leaders, teams, companies, and even across business ecosystems.

Notes

1 Trei, L. (2007, February 7). New study yields instructive results on how mindset affects learning. *Stanford Report*. Retrieved from http://news.stanford.edu/news/2007/february7/dweck-020707.html
2 Siroya, S. (2016). A smart loan for people with no credit history (yet) [Video File]. Retrieved from https://www.ted.com/talks/shivani_siroya_a_smart_loan_for_people_with_no_credit_history_yet
3 Martin, R. (2009). *The opposable mind: How successful leaders win through integrative thinking*. Boston, MA: Harvard Business School Publishing.
4 Opam, K. (2015, March 17). Silicon Valley's diversity problem followed it to SXSW. *The Verge*. Retrieved from www.theverge.com/2015/3/17/8236905/sxsw-2015-diversity-race-gender-silicon-valley
5 Martin, R. (2009). *The opposable mind: How successful leaders win through integrative thinking*. Boston, MA: Harvard Business School Publishing.
6 Kalanithi, P. (2016). *When breath becomes air*. New York, NY: Penguin Random House, p. 170.
7 Rich, N. (2016, January 6). The lawyer who became DuPont's worst nightmare. *The New York Times Magazine*.
8 Mordock, J. (2017, February 13). DuPont, Chemours to pay $670 million over PFOA suits. *USA Today*. Retrieved from www.usatoday.com/story/news/2017/02/13/dupont-and-chemours-pay-670m-settle-pfoa-litigation/97842870/

5 Future-proofing your leadership

Beyond a shared mindset, there is one other similarity among the leaders I talked to while writing this book: There are no "chosen ones." Of course, some people display an adventurous growth mindset earlier on than others. But most future first leaders I've known weren't born that way. Almost all of them recalled events and personal experiences that led to some type of mindset shift. For some of them the shift was sudden; for others a slow transformation occurred while they were working with more traditional business models.

Second, this transformation is not a one-off occurrence—one day you wake up future first. It has to be sustained with an ongoing commitment to future-proofing your company, innovatively approaching challenges, and understanding your role within a larger ecosystem. This chapter will look at how leaders transition themselves and their organizations to a future first mindset.

Embracing innovation challenges

Business leaders are constantly challenged to innovate within the limits of profitability. Any idea for a new product line or service is eventually thrown out if it doesn't demonstrate the potential for generating profit margins. What if the limitations of sustainably producing products and services using finite material resources, while reducing waste and pollution, were also approached as an innovation challenge? The possibilities for inventing and reinventing your company's core business model could be expanded to encompass both profitability and sustainability.

Case study: digital transition at print-based institution

When I consulted over ten years ago with one of the most highly regarded international newspapers in the world, its leaders were struggling with deep uncertainty over their future. The newspaper industry was in a massive upheaval driven by internet news sources. The leadership was in a crisis mode. They were being forced to shift their business model from one in which most of their revenue came from print advertising to an unknown future centered on the online newspaper. Digital advertising revenue couldn't replace the losses in print advertising revenue.

Another obstacle for them: Newspapers turn out a new product every single day. They have longer "think pieces" but ultimately make their money by staying current. The path to future success was very murky at the time.

Today, the preeminent newspaper's website and other online services are among the best in its industry. The company's successful transition was partly due to their leaders' commitment to innovation in the midst of a volatile and uncertain business environment. The CEO of business operations had built a strong capability around future-proofing the company by investing heavily in their strategic planning team. They hired Harvard MBAs to do broad market research, talk with customers and employees from across departments, and run scenarios on the future of print and digital media. Based on these deep dive analyses, they decided to close one of their printing plants. And they decided to integrate the print and digital newsrooms, staff, and office buildings, all of which had been separate up until then.

They viewed readership trends as innovation challenges: How can we adapt to serve the technologically and socially dynamic preferences of our younger readership? They also took their solid base of older readers into account, and accurately foresaw that it wasn't just going to be younger readers who preferred to read the news online. Middle-aged readers would change their habits in response to the explosion of new digital media options. While not necessarily the intention of the transition to digital media, reading the newspaper online saves trees and materials otherwise used to make newsprint as well as gas and energy used to print and distribute the physical newspaper.

The result of all these efforts? A transition to digital media that maintained their brand as the gold standard in journalism—an even more difficult accomplishment in an ocean of digital media voices.

Switching your mindset out of the present tense

Presentism—the widespread inability to accurately forecast or think about the future—is a behavior encouraged both by culture, such as an unrelenting 24-hour news cycle, and by some very fundamental cognitive functions. While most companies see at least some value in analyzing future trends, transforming your organization's core functions to align with these trends has proved easier said than done. When leaders and companies do succeed, it can be the result of an epiphany or a sustained, intelligent effort.

Case study: fixing a fashion disaster

Fashion entrepreneur Eileen Fisher's transformation started after a 2012 trip to China. "I had just come back from two back-to-back conferences," said Fisher. "I was tired, but there was a company sustainability meeting off-site. I was supposed to go."[1]

In fact, Fisher was likely exhausted. She had started the company with a $400 loan. By 2012, it had grown to a $300 million company with eight hundred employees. Her clothes were known for their simplicity but, like most large apparel companies, her products went through a complicated supply chain. Raw materials were shipped from one country, dyed in another, and manufactured in a third location before being shipped back to the US. Fisher had already realized there was one big problem with this manufacturing process: it was remarkably polluting. After all, as Fisher notes, the negative environmental impact of apparel is second only to that of the oil industry.

Among the biggest issues is the huge amount of water used to grow cotton. A striking example is that, in the 1950s, Soviet bureaucrats diverted the rivers in Kazakhstan that fed into the Aral Sea in order to irrigate cotton fields. Over the past sixty years, the Aral has gone from being one of the four largest lakes in the world to a dry bed with only a small remnant of its western edge remaining. Abandoned former fishing villages and boats sit in the middle of a desert, eerie reminders of the devastation ultimately created by cotton clothing.

The pollution and damage caused by clothing production is perhaps surprising to consumers, but hardly a secret to those in the industry. For Fisher, this was no longer acceptable. So, just home from China, she forced herself to pack her bags and go to the sustainability meeting. "You could feel a lot of energy building around all this great work that was happening," said Fisher. "I thought: 'I have to do this. I don't care if I'm tired. This really matters.'"

The weekend was inspiring. Fisher's changing mindset about her business was cemented in a new commitment. "Amazing work was happening there. This is where the Vision 2020 came out."[2]

Vision 2020 is designed to improve the environmental impact of Eileen Fisher's clothing lines by using all organic cotton and linen, reducing chemicals used in dyes, and reducing waste material and shipping, among other measures. "It wasn't my idea," Fisher said. "But I wanted to make a radical commitment that we would make all of our clothes sustainable by 2020."[3]

Every other decision-maker in the apparel industry knows that their products cause pollution. Most of them probably also know that business-as-usual could only lead to an increasing number of tragedies like the Aral or the poisoning of even more rivers in China and Southeast Asia. So why do most leaders ignore their responsibility in all this? Why did Fisher confront the pollution head on? The critical difference is in how industry leaders deal with future events. Most leaders push huge problems off into the future. Fisher could no longer pretend that the future was a different place. She overcame the presentism that prevented other industry leaders from taking action.

In taking definitive action to commit to cleaning up her clothing line, Fisher shared several traits in common with other leaders who overcome presentism. She was clear-sighted and open-minded about the future trends in technology, energy, and demographics that affect her business. For example, she knew that techno-logical innovation could allow her to use cleaner dyes. She sought to make sense of the trends that are most relevant and material to future-proofing her business by viewing them through her understanding of top global challenges. For Fisher, part of this was the future of water scarcity. Without improvements in apparel practices, there will be a huge gap between the supply and demand for affordable, fresh water. Neither people nor the apparel industry will have enough.

Finally, she prioritized what future trends were most important for her to understand deeply. In any given industry, it is easy to be overwhelmed by a sea of information. On the one hand, fashion is, by nature, constantly changing. But it also has a negative material impact on the world and often relies on crowded labor conditions. If you don't try to understand all of this, you could become paralyzed in the present—unable to act boldly on what matters most.

Leading for the future

Once we are conscious of the negative impact of presentism, we can begin pushing back. We can ask questions that help us approach the future in useful ways. We can develop specific business processes and skills that foster regular reflection on our company's most important future trends. Over time, these questions will help us move toward a dynamic future first mindset.

What are the top three to five material issues most critical to your business performance now and over the next five to ten years?

Eileen Fisher might say water availability, cotton production practices, and the toxicity of fabric dye chemicals. None of these is a secret in her industry. But asking this question is the first step in really focusing on issues that will almost certainly be part of your company's future. In most apparel companies, it's likely that only a few people in the company were tasked with regularly thinking about what kind of chemicals would be in the dye in ten years. As CEO, it would have been easy for Eileen Fisher herself to have spent most of her time in the immediate present tense, like getting out her autumn collection by June. Of course, she has to think about the immediate issues of running a business, but she needs a platform to begin to look at the future at the same time.

Similarly, executives at an industrial company like Ingersoll Rand might spend days thinking about how to make their distribution warehouses smarter or provide incentives for natural refrigerants. But when they asked this simple question about business performance, they found that greenhouse gas emissions were the number one materiality issue for them. This was true both in their products and in how they could impact their customers. Then they had a vantage point that would allow them to move out of the daily noise of presentism and prioritize their future goals.

What data does your company already obtain on materiality issues and future trends?

Now that you've got a starting point, look at where this data came from. How are you collecting it? How often? One common trap is only looking at data on current customers and products. To take on future challenges, design your innovation, and gain new customers, this is not enough. Here's a traditional business example. Eileen Fisher is known for her loose, flowing designs. Recognizing the need to attract a younger demographic, she experimented with a more form-fitting t-shirt, but has to further capture a younger customer segment to become more sustainable. In the case of clothes, mobility, electronics, and experimentation are the best ways to get data on what new customers want. A less traditional example is her investment in using more organic cotton and fewer toxic dyes. It's higher risk, but potentially even higher reward.

How is the best data on future trends used in any business decision-making process?

This is closing the loop. What if Eileen Fisher had decided she was too tired to attend the sustainability conference? What would that have meant for all the work that ended up becoming the industry-leading Vision 2020?

This can happen at any company. R&D at an electronics manufacturer could gather data from eighteen- to thirty-year-olds suggesting that they want all their personal electronics to be wearable and remain charged all day. R&D prototypes a wearable that functions as a voice-activated phone, e-wallet, and car keys. But all executive attention is focused on a merger, an ongoing lawsuit and rolling out the 2018 products. If the innovation doesn't make it up to the top leadership until mid-2018, the R&D work is essentially lost no matter which way the electronics market breaks.

There are several steps to transitioning out of presentism for leaders and companies. But ultimately, executive teams and boards of directors must get the powerful information they need on the top materiality issues and future trends to make strategic decisions, as well as ongoing choices about investments in innovative product design, production innovation, and people practices.

Adopting integrative thinking

Since the start of the twenty-first century, hybrid cars have become successful by offering some of the benefits of gas and electric engines. Leadership books have extolled the value of pivoting to new strategies. Even sports like basketball are becoming more "positionless," with a premium placed on players who can fill three or even four of the traditional five positions. Despite all the value produced by flexibility, business models—and thinking—are still more likely to fit firmly into categories like "for-profit" or "non-profit." Learning how to think in a more integrative manner is critical for leaders who want to create profitable businesses that also innovate around huge environmental and social challenges.

Case study: building hybrid impact

For a few leaders, transitioning to an integrative mindset comes relatively easily. For most of the 1980s and into the 1990s, a civil war ravaged Guatemala. Among the hardest hit groups were the indigenous Mayan communities in the mountainous northern part of the country. In the late 1990s, a few members of the community formed a coffee-growing cooperative called Cooperative Maya Ixil to help their families begin to rebuild their lives and community.

In 2005, the cooperative received a $50,000 loan from Root Capital, a social impact fund that supports small-scale farmers and their businesses throughout Africa and Latin America. Among other benefits, the financing allowed the cooperative to pay their members promptly. By 2015, the Maya Ixil had grown to 175 farmers and its need for financing increased as well; the cooperative now has access to a $450,000 line of credit from Root Capital. This is the kind of positive story that every social investor would like to be able to tell. But Root Capital was able to make it happen by developing their integrative thinking.

I've worked with Root Capital along with a number of other hybrid organizations. Since its founding in 1999, Root Capital has operated in the gray area between traditional philanthropy and mainstream commercial markets. The organization is funded by impact investors, who are often willing to accept a below market-rate of return (about 2 percent) in exchange for having social and environmental impact investments in their portfolio. Root Capital also receives a good portion of their funding from traditional philanthropic donors.

This organizational thinking did not always come easily. In 2016, the executive team at Root Capital realized that, like many hybrid organizations, their stakeholders were polarized around financial and social impact—some represented a financially driven business view and others were more exclusively focused on social impact. Their CEO decided to explicitly state that their #1 leadership competency would be: "An integrative mindset that brings commitment and experimentation to increasing social impact and financial results." Now they look for this integrative mindset when they hire new staff, and they cultivate integrative thinking skills throughout the organization. Through their hybrid model, Root Capital is tackling a huge risky market made up of many small- and medium-sized agricultural businesses that, given the resources they need to grow, can provide livelihoods for millions of people living in poverty.

Leading through integration

For most of us, integrative thinking is more difficult. But it can be developed by building high levels of trust and respect for differences, so they can be expressed, heard, and considered. Executive teams can start by reflecting on their team dynamics with a few challenging questions.

How much does everyone speak up? How much does everyone listen to each other's ideas and differences? How good are we at mining the ideas of everyone on the team?

We've all been in many business meetings that are dominated by a few vocal people and where others are obviously stifling their opinions. Many business leaders have succeeded by being very attached to their views and very vocal about them. Others have succeeded by not speaking up too openly about their true views and opinions.

People sense when the best ideas are not being heard or decisions are made based on who is the loudest about their views. But most teams don't know how to get out of these dysfunctional dynamics.

Case study: bringing it all back home

For me, the most dramatic—and, in retrospect, most endearing—experience I had with challenging team dynamics was working with a family-owned business. The board was solely made up of family members, and I was facilitating. The board meetings were often very heated with at least one person being very quiet. But this family business was just a more out-in-the-open example of a common leadership challenge. The same dynamics exist to some degree or another even when the members aren't caught up in a disagreement. They all get in the way of having more productive meetings driven by integrative thinking.

It is impossible to adopt an integrative mindset with these dynamics guiding interactions. One powerful technique for aligning an executive team or a board of directors around integrative thinking is to ask every team member to balance the time they spend in each meeting advocating for their own views and perspectives, and inquiring and asking questions about the views of others. A facilitator can use a timer and actively engage in building everyone's skills for balancing advocacy and inquiry, which is the foundation for integrative thinking.

What decisions do we make that are the most polarizing to the team? What happens when these topics are discussed?

In some meetings, polarizing differences among team members push people to take more extreme views. Worse, these views are often couched in the language of rational business arguments. But underneath people can sense the unspoken power dynamics, individual needs, and genuine differences in people's values or sense of purpose in their jobs.

Integrative mindsets explore empathy for differences. One technique is to ask executives to play devil's advocate on their own views and take the view that is contrary to their own position. This can build empathy. But just as importantly, the technique can reveal how arguments are usually constructed with only part of the data, which leads to a fixed mindset rather than a future first growth mindset.

Expanding the values in all business decisions

Most business decisions are presented in the language of financial benefits and drawbacks. What are the strategic advantages of this decision? Will this product increase market share? Despite this familiar language, other values and even emotions get baked into all decisions as well. But while it may be OK to talk about heartbreak or joy or fear in our personal lives, we generally tend to avoid using emotional language at work because it is considered unprofessional—or distracting from the "real issues." However, understanding all the values in a decision—or a company—often requires more emotional language to be used. We aren't exactly flying blind, but we often have one eye closed. Leaders can start being more explicit about the values inherent in their decisions by asking good questions.

How rational is any business decision?

On the first page of Daniel Kahneman's bestselling book, *Thinking Fast and Slow*[4], there are two images. In the first image is a picture of a woman looking angrily at the camera with her mouth open. In the other image is a multiplication problem. According to Kahneman, a Nobel Prize–winning behavioral economist and cognitive psychologist, the way we process this information shows two distinct types of thinking. With the picture, we use an intuitive automatic and largely unconscious system. We can quickly and easily determine that the woman is very upset and perhaps about to loudly share some choice words.

The math problem engages a whole different part of our brain, one that is analytical, deliberative, and largely conscious. Looking at 24×17 prompts us to remember how to do this problem from school and realize it would be easier with paper. Without paper, we start working it out in our head, straining to remember one set of numbers while multiplying the other. Our bodies even tense up slightly while solving the problem.

In our daily lives, we are constantly toggling back and forth between these two types of thinking. Neither system represents a better way to think. Clearly, we need both, and for Kahneman, both have unique value. You wouldn't want to use an unconscious, intuitive mode to fill out a medical form. Similarly, it's probably a waste of time to read body language using purely analytic techniques. More to the point, it's virtually impossible to only use your analytical side. Before you start to think "that person's voice is more high-pitched than normal, they are speaking loudly and over-enunciating syllables and their breathing seems a little tight," you will already know that he or she is excited. You can't suppress the intuitive side that reads emotions.

There are two important points here. First, we need to realize that we have two useful information processing systems. Second, we need to realize that not every situation will require just one system. Answering maths questions is clearly a job for analytic, conscious thinking. But most decisions we make are more complicated and not nearly as neatly defined as the book examples.

Imagine you are in an investor meeting with a startup. They are requesting an initial round of funding and present their financials and business plan. The numbers don't quite add up, but the people you meet with are engaging and confident and the information they leave with you comes in a very attractive portfolio. Whatever your final decision is, you should realize that you will be weighing subjective values like the appearance and impression of the people and their products with the hard numbers they gave you. And the harder you try to pretend that your decision is purely based on analytics, the more likely you are to misunderstand how you arrived at your decision.

The truth is that every decision is values-based. You go out to buy one blender but come back with a more expensive one—not for the added features but because you liked the color. You doubt someone's knowledge of Euro-league basketball because they keep stuttering and avoiding your eyes—not because you know any better. Often when we think we've made rational decisions, we've actually been heavily influenced by unconscious, subjective, and emotional values. In some cases, we just end up with an over-priced blender. But this confusion about how we are making decisions can be much more high-stakes. Consider something as basic and important as annual salaries, which are statistically higher for people who are subjectively considered more attractive. According to one study, companies decide to pay an average of $230,000 more to better-looking people over the course of their lifetimes.[5]

Nowhere is this more true than in business. There are an increasing number of businesses that claim to be purpose-driven or are changing their practices for environmental reasons. But the overwhelming logic of business decision-making is still maximizing profits or shareholder value. Businesses use all sorts of tools to make rational decisions—like evaluating financial implications or resource investments. But, despite their best efforts to hermetically seal decision-making from subjective and emotional issues, these values keep popping up. Businesses think they are making rational decisions, but attempting to eliminate the unconscious, subjective, and emotional aspects is futile. As Kahneman showed, we have two decision systems running, whether we want to or not. Many leaders assume they are making rational decisions by suppressing the subjective mode. Instead they are setting themselves up for terrible decision outcomes.

Case study: another word for "mistake"

In 2002, I worked on implementing JPMorgan Chase's $5 billion outsourcing deal with IBM to roll out an "on-demand" technology strategy over seven years. The plan was for IBM to take over managing data centers, help desks, distributed computing, and voice networks. Several thousand of the technology staff internal to the bank switched over to become IBM staff, while other people were let go to have their jobs taken over by IBM's partners in India.

Two years later, JPMorgan merged with Bank One and Jamie Dimon, who was the successor to the CEO, took over the major leadership decisions. Soon thereafter, JPMorgan announced that the bank would cancel the remainder of the contract and bring 4,000 tech support staff back in house. One of the reasons cited was that the CIO of the newly merged bank was more of a "do it yourself guy." We called the process "re-insourcing." It was expensive, disruptive, and provided relatively little obvious net benefit to the bank.

If, at any given moment, you had asked any of the executives involved in the processes—including me—why these decisions were being made, we could have showed you reams of data and presentations. Very smart people were involved all along the way. Plenty of rational arguments supported both the outsourcing and re-insourcing. But each decision also had multiple other values associated with it. There were subjective values associated with the quality and ownership of the IT services. There were emotions around the people involved. In the early 2000s, there was less data and more fear surrounding outsourcing IT. There was also a much larger stigma attached to operating off-shore call centers in India.

As with any major decision, leadership dynamics and personal beliefs were involved at every step, but they were largely unrecognized. When people explained why they were doing things a certain way, they explained it in rational business terms. But they ended up with a decision that in retrospect seems ambiguous. I don't know if recognizing the subjective values in the decision-making process would necessarily have eliminated all the expenses involved. The whole process was too complicated to make accurate projections. But it would certainly have made the messy process more transparent.

Leading with understanding of all values

What are your top five to eight most important business decisions? What explicit language could you use to identify the different types of values that go into and come out of these decisions?

One example of an important business decision is letting people go because of a performance issue or a merger or downsizing. Leaders can attempt to create rational business processes for managing these challenging decisions, but they cannot stamp out the values and emotions involved in letting people go for any reason.

Who are the major stakeholders of the decision? What information do they need and want to know?

You have different stakeholder views in the process of letting people go. Executive leaders may want to know that performance issues are being addressed in compliance with HR standards. Or they may want to know that the downsizing is meeting certain financial goals.

What analytic data is required to make and implement the decision? What subjective data is required?

When people are let go for performance issues or laid off for downsizing, employees want to know that the decisions were made in the most analytical and deliberative way in order to view the decisions as fair and just. You have to show people that you have used a deliberative data-driven process that was fair so that the people left behind remain committed to the organization. If HR tries to overly distance themselves from people emotionally when they have to be laid off, this can lead to bitterness, and even lawsuits later on.

What we need to avoid is pretending we can make purely rational decisions. To a lesser or greater extent, all decisions are values-based. Ignoring that fact sets your company up for making bad choices without knowing why. It limits your employees' abilities. In the worst cases, it also sets the table for people to make socially and sometimes financially destructive choices.

Ecosystems: no business is an island

In the mid-twentieth century, it was easy for large businesses to imagine themselves as stand-alone entities—like corporate islands with discrete boundaries. Today business is much messier. Companies have outsourced manufacturing and customer support. They manage brands across a variety of international climates and multiple channels and platforms. Computers and the internet have sped up data management and decision-making by many times. We need a new language to describe this world.

"Systems" are organisms comprised of a complex array of relationships. They can be naturally occurring entities or human creations. Academics, including biologists, economists, and psychologists, have also found the concept of the system useful to describe a more interconnected world. Organizational psychologists use the idea of the system to better understand corporations and how to optimize their effectiveness.

In contrast to the relatively simple business structures of yesteryear, today's corporation is a complex non-linear type of system. The classic organizational chart shows decision-making flowing from the CEO and board down to other executives and then on to middle management. If you were to map the decision-making within a contemporary corporation, you would typically see a networked structure made out of a series of connected hubs and spokes.

The image would resemble those maps that airlines put in the back of their in-flight magazines. United Airlines, for example, has a map of the US superimposed with lines tracing everywhere they fly. There are a number of busy clusters, hubs like San Francisco, Washington, DC, and Chicago. But the hubs also shoot off hundreds of lines, or spokes, to individual cities. The networked system is a busy picture; it may even appear chaotic. The old vertical hierarchical organizational model is much more static and easier to understand. But it has little to do with how businesses work today.

A traditional systems view of business performance has similar shortcomings. It aimed to align the company's interconnected elements, such as the strategy, structure, talent, processes, metrics, and rewards from Jay Galbraith's Star Model.[6] The common assumption was that the key to driving organizational effectiveness and performance results was to align all of these internal elements with the external environment through a sound strategy. At the same time each internal element had to be aligned with the others. It is still important in today's networked corporate system to develop internal congruence between the company's strategic priorities and the organizational structure, or between the leadership's talents and the abilities required to successfully perform these executive roles.

The challenge with the systems' view of today's corporations is that they are networked within larger systems. As a result, there is no fixed boundary between what is internal and external to companies anymore. Instead, corporations have highly interdependent relationships with the larger systems surrounding them. They are embedded within wider cultures and societies, as well as economies, governments, and ecosystems. Today's corporations take many more resources out of these larger systems. They have a larger and much more powerful impact across the ecosystems where they operate.

Reimagining mobility

During Tesla's rise, Elon Musk has become a bit of a celebrity CEO. He has been the subject of innumerable admiring profiles and appeared as a guest on late night TV shows. But despite his image as a tech superman, neither he nor Tesla is acting alone. Fortunately, Musk seems to have this concept embedded in his mindset and business practices. For example, Tesla makes all of their designs open-source—anyone who is using them in good faith is allowed to work with the designs, hopefully improving on them.

This mindset is important because, though there will always be CEOs who stand out for some reason or another, neither Musk nor anyone else can shift the world to a solar-based economy by their own heroic actions. This holds true for any effort to take on massive global challenges. Instead, future first leadership always fosters collaboration within a larger ecosystem. Tesla, for example, entered the auto ecosystem by upping the ante with Toyota and Porsche for alternative drivetrain cars. The company's success reverberated through the market. Partially in response, GM is now introducing a mid-priced all-electric vehicle.

Telsa, meanwhile, has entered a partnership with another nascent player in the car ecosystem. Google and Tesla are developing software for self-driving electric cars. The result has been a focus on autonomous technology by traditional carmakers. In 2016, GM bought Cruise, a self-driving startup, for an estimated $1 billion.[7]

But Tesla wasn't the only one embracing non-traditional business models in the car industry. Among other companies, BMW and Mercedes Benz have invested in or purchased their own car sharing services. Zipcar was bought by Avis, the car rental company. In response to the interest in car sharing, Ford introduced an option for new Ford owners to help pay off their loans by renting the vehicles.[8] Meanwhile, GM targeted car sharing that relied on cars driven by their new Cruise technology.

The result? Elon Musk, formerly a skeptic of car sharing, announced in 2016 that Tesla would begin a program in which Tesla owners could pay off cars by using an improved self-driving function.[9] The change in direction keeps with Tesla's broader plan. Depending on its growth, ride sharing combined with autonomous electric vehicles will lead to a substantial reduction in carbon emissions.

The bigger point is that, while Tesla is often on the tech vanguard, they must also react to other innovations within the ecosystem.

Leading in an ecosystem-based future

Business leaders need to bring commitment and collaboration to go beyond the outdated approach of "one-company, one-leader at a time." To really grow this mindset, they need to hold strategic conversations with their executive teams about having a deliberate impact on their business ecosystem. These might sound a bit like a strategic planning meeting for a whole business ecosystem.

What are the big external goals you want your companies to achieve over the next five to ten years within the larger business ecosystems in which they operate?

A future first goal could be as big as redefining the future of cars, energy, agriculture, or water. Or it could be as simple as making the company's facilities carbon emissions neutral within the next five years. But don't avoid setting a goal just because it seems too big—or too small.

Who are your potential partners within your business ecosystem? This may be your competitors, regulators, or investors, and what problems do you want to solve together. Who do you want to involve in your ecosystem?

For example, companies like PayPal that started off as an alternative form of payment to banks have to be more than frenemies with banks now. Banks are important partners that will help PayPal redefine the relationship between money and consumers.

What can you collaborate on with your competitors, and what do you need to continue to compete on?

For example, in apparel, the big companies have created coalitions to detoxify the materials and manufacturing processes. But they still compete on product design.

Trade-offs are not the only answer

In the best-case scenario, the future first leaders who fundamentally transform the private sector will enable future generations to look back at the trade-offs we once made as part of business-as-usual with bewilderment and sympathy. Rhodes scholar and previous director at the White House Council on Environmental Quality, Maria Blair, confided to me, "My biggest fear is that on my deathbed, my girls will say to me, 'Mom, why didn't you do more to stop climate change? How hard would it have been to give up a few more things for us?'"

I deeply echo Maria's concern, and I've heard many smart successful business people say that they feel the same way. When I look at my children and observe other people's children, my mind constantly leaps forward to the future we're leaving for them, and what we can do to change our global outcomes.

Nothing is more important to the future of our world and the next generation than for business leaders to shift to a future first mindset. Business leaders are more aware than ever before of global challenges like climate change, water and food shortages, and social dynamism, and are taking important steps to address these challenges. Every single one of them needs to act in a way that is going to create innovative solutions that generate future value for the next generation's environment and society. What distinguishes future first business leaders is their resolve and capacity to act boldly on their values and opportunities for innovation—and that is what the world needs most from the private sector right now.

Checklist #1. Developing your future first mindset as a leader

- ☐ Learn to hear your distinct voice of presentism. Identify the potential gains and losses of focusing on the present.
- ☐ Remind yourself of the goals and values of your future first mindset. What are the potential gains and losses of investing in these goals and values?
- ☐ What are the trade-offs of investing in the present versus the future? What are the pay-offs?
- ☐ Take future first actions, and observe and learn from the outcomes.

Checklist #2. Developing future first mindset as an executive team

- ☐ Determine the most materially important issues and trends affecting your company.
- ☐ Set up effective processes to get timely relevant data on these issues and trends at the top leadership level.
- ☐ Determine the most critical business decisions you need to make. What are the data, logic, and analysis, as well as the judgment required to make these critical business decisions?
- ☐ What are the social and emotional implications of these trends for your stakeholders? What is the data you need on these implications and how could you get it?
- ☐ Make it common practice in your meetings with the executive team and board of directors to ask people to balance their time advocating their views and inquiring about the views of others.
- ☐ Ask your team to seek out evidence that challenges their conclusions. Require that people use careful analysis instead of statistical intuitions.

☐ Decide what ecosystem your business will play in. Define at least one big goal you will achieve in that ecosystem.

☐ Decide who you will collaborate with and what you will collaborate on, as well as what you will compete on, within your business ecosystem.

Notes

1 Editors (2015, June). Eileen Fisher: How finding her personal purpose inspired a new direction for her company. *Conscious Company*, 3, 60–68.
2 Ibid.
3 Ibid.
4 Kahneman, D. (2011). *Thinking fast and slow*. New York, NY: Farrar, Straus, Giroux.
5 Shellenbarger, S. (2011, October). On the job beauty is more than skin-deep. Retrieved from www.wsj.com/articles/SB10001424052970203687504576655331418204842.
6 Galbraith, J. (2014). *Designing organizations: Strategy, structure, and process at the business and enterprise level*, 3rd ed. San Francisco, CA: Jossey-Bass.
7 Primack, D. and Korosec K. (2016, March 11). GM buying self-driving tech startup for more than $1billion. *Fortune*. Retrieved from http://fortune.com/2016/03/11/gm-buying-self-driving-tech-startup-for-more-than-1-billion/.
8 Risen, T. (2015, June 25). Amid rise of Zipcar and Uber, Ford drives into car sharing space. *US News*. Retrieved from www.usnews.com/news/articles/2015/06/25/ford-car-sharing-program-shows-demand-for-zipcar-uber
9 DeBord, M. (2016, July 23). Elon Musk is on the verge of making a huge change for Tesla's owners. *Business Insider*. Retrieved from www.businessinsider.com/musk-tesla-car-sharing-2016-7

6   Building future first DNA into
    Etsy, Apple, and Nike

In April 2003, teams of scientists working around the world completed one of the greatest biological feats ever. They had created a complete map of the human genome, the complex combinations of amino acids central to the development of every human. Reading from this "book of life" helps doctors understand the genetic basis for over five thousand medical conditions. It allows pharmaceutical researchers to create drugs targeting, for example, cancerous tumors.

Mapping out organizational DNA—the common set of behaviors and core capabilities at the heart of a company—has similar benefits for leaders. It gives insight into the distinct set of qualities that determines a company's performance, deficiencies, and possible cures. But understanding the code behind how a company functions also provides an additional advantage. As humans, we are generally stuck with our biologically determined height, eye color, and predisposition for a certain kind of cancer. A company can improve its strategy, structure, measurements, and rewards.

We've already seen how future first leaders share a similar mindset. But their impact will be greatly expanded if they can transfer these common ways of thinking and acting to an entire organization. There is no one generic formulation of "correct DNA" that will always replicate the perfect organization for every business sector, mission, existing structure, and so on. But successful future first companies are ones in which certain behaviors take hold and become repeated capabilities: embracing innovation as a sustainability challenge, developing integrative thinking, overcoming presentism, expanding the values that drive business decisions, and moving beyond one-leader and one-company.

Introducing these capabilities across whole organizations will look very different depending on the company's strategy and stage of development. Generally speaking, there are additional challenges with larger and more developed companies. As leaders begin to pivot these organizations toward future first priorities, they encounter institutional inertia. They are, essentially, trying to retrofit capabilities into companies that were designed from a very different set of DNA. The obstacles to organizational change are built into every element of the company, including their structures, processes, leadership and talent.

Small companies have the opposite problem. They often have nowhere near the financial resources as bigger companies, but can change directions or focus quickly. Newer, smaller companies that want to change their DNA are typically more agile. In fact, all the small companies I look at in this book actually began with future first goals. But no matter what size the company is now, its challenge is to develop organizational DNA that can be scaled as it makes a net positive material impact while expanding its value frontier.

Embracing innovation challenges

Corporate sustainability has been traditionally saddled with the assumption of added expenses and sacrifices to product design and quality. But, future first companies are seeing the business opportunity to solve for the dual challenge of achieving both profitability and sustainability through innovation. As you read in Chapter 3, Nike's enormous success with the flyknit shoe came from investing heavily in product innovation until they found a new way to make a shoe that both reduced the amount of unsustainable material used and increased the performance of the athlete wearing the shoe. But how does Nike uniquely approach the process of innovation?

Case study: Nike's counterintuitive approach to large-scale innovation

In the typical innovation brainstorming session, everyone is encouraged to "put all their ideas in front of the room." There are no bad ideas—sort of like preschool art class. Then the group votes with sticky dots or a group conversation on their favorite ideas. When the session ends, there are about five to ten new ideas that get researched further with real data in the best-case scenario. All the other ideas are usually forgotten.

This is not how Nike's DNA is coded. Noah Murphy-Reinhertz works in the heart of Nike's famous innovation kitchen. In an interview, Murphy-Reinhertz told me that Nike's approach to innovation is an extension of their core business. Nike products are used by teams, but they are primarily designed to support the performance of the individual athlete. Nike invests heavily in innovation with a corporate team of over one thousand employees. This team goes out to meet directly with athletes and get product feedback at all stages of development.

From LeBron James to Cristiano Ronaldo to Tiger Woods to Serena Williams, Nike is programmed with the idea that exceptional athletes succeed because of individual perseverance. This DNA is the same code that is pushed out into innovation. Instead of group-think and consensus, the company is structured to allow anyone on the innovation team to pursue a new idea, even if everyone else on the team pooh-poohs it. All they have to do is persevere. They're even encouraged to try again if they fail with their idea. Nike's capability for innovation emanates from a DNA aligned with their core business of enhancing the performance of the exceptional individual.

If there is one way in which Nike's approach to innovation is similar to most other big companies, it's in the resources they have available. GE or Ford or Pixar may approach innovation differently, but all of them can afford to support a team of people whose only job is to come up with ideas for the future. Smaller companies don't have this luxury, but they do have different advantages, such as the speed and scrappiness to quickly try out new ideas and innovations without taking resources away from their core business.

Case study: Etsy and the challenges of innovation in a startup

In the mid-2000s, two twenty-something roommates in Brooklyn had a conversation that went something like this:

> "Hey, I'm starting this website—you want to work with me?"
> "Okay. What do you want me to do? I'm not a programmer."
> "You can be the marketing guy."
> "I don't know anything about marketing."
> "Then you'll be perfect."

Just like that, professional guitarist Matt Stinchcomb became marketing director at a handmade crafts retail website called Etsy. The company didn't have any of the resources of a Nike. They only had a handful of employees—they certainly couldn't hire twenty people to brainstorm what the crafts e-commerce environment would look like in five or ten years. But when your company's senior leadership is two roommates—the founder was Robert Kalin, a classics major and woodworker—you are extremely nimble. You don't have to worry about existing relationships with clients or communicating with thousands of employees about new policy or if the new baseball cleats are on schedule. You just do.

This is what Etsy did. In the early years, nearly everything about the business ran contrary to traditional business practice. As Etsy grew, new employees were added because they seemed interesting or were already friends with Kalin or Stinchcomb. Performance metrics were virtually non-existent. "In the very beginning," said Stinchcomb, "we didn't really even know how much stuff was being sold. It was pretty loosey-goosey."

For a number of years, none of these organizational idiosyncrasies mattered. Etsy kept growing astronomically because, like any good business, Kalin and Stinchcomb had found a need in the marketplace. The idea of linking buyers and sellers via the web was hardly new. Ten years earlier, eBay had become a surprise success out of the first wave of internet companies. Amazon offers direct internet access to nearly every in-production consumer commodity. eBay then allowed peer-to-peer sales of a wider variety of often used or out-of-stock items.

But by 2005, the typical online consumer experience felt impersonal and unsatisfying to many people. Etsy offered an alternative. Instead of ordering from the pile of mass-produced electronics and clothes, Etsy users could surf through the world's best vintage and craft stores. Then Etsy was able to fine-tune this idea by guaranteeing something missing in this transaction: authenticity. In short, Etsy was innovating an entirely new market. Like other startups, they were largely able to succeed with one good idea and some venture capital. Their DNA was fully aligned with future first innovation and other capabilities. But, as we will see, their success soon brought lots of growing pains.

Overcoming presentism

The Buddhist adage to "live in the present" has become commonly accepted wisdom in our culture, even in the business world where mindfulness gurus coach Silicon Valley executives. Through technology, media, and entertainment, our attention has been captured by the allure of the now. It is no surprise that business performance is narrowly measured in quarterly profit cycles.

But the benefits of concentrated attention in the present assume that people have a strong foundation in understanding history and the implications of the present for the future. Future first leaders and companies invest in the capabilities to overcome presentism by constantly examining the past and forecasting and responding to future trends.

Case study: PepsiCo and the challenges of a less bad future

In interviews, CEO Indra Nooyi is very forward-thinking and sincere about her desire to transform PepsiCo into a leader in healthy snacks for the future. She is also a talented, committed executive. But she faces an uphill slog in her efforts for one principal reason: Her company's DNA is far from future first aligned. Not surprisingly for a one-hundred-year-old company, PepsiCo has a traditional corporate structure that complements its mission in food and beverages. The company has strong capabilities in distribution, organizational efficiency, and brand management. But these capabilities aren't enough to support Nooyi's future first efforts. She may be the single most powerful executive in the company, but until she transforms PepsiCo's organizational DNA, the company will only be able to walk, rather than run, toward the future.

Nooyi has had some successes, such as removing aspartame, a sweetener associated with a variety of health problems,[1] from Diet Pepsi. She has also been successful in helping to cut trillions of empty calories from the American diet, but her flagship products still contribute to, for example, mass diabetes among low-income populations.

Nooyi's situation is common for the heads of many large companies attempting organizational change. The problem isn't just that it's hard to move such big pieces around—although that doesn't help. The leaders have a fundamental problem in advancing future first initiatives: They are naturally backwards-facing. PepsiCo has built up its enormous brand value over the course of a century.

The flagship product of the company—fizzy, sweet, brownish water—is virtually worthless without the brand. The same can be said of other PepsiCo snack products, such as triangular corn chips covered in orange flavor dust or bottles of tap water. Without the brands "Doritos" and "Aquafina" slapped on them, they would only demand a fraction of their retail value. As a result, the number one job of the majority of PepsiCo's employees is to protect what they've already done: maintain their brand's value. This is not to say that PepsiCo has no interest in repositioning their existing brands or creating new brands. It just means that, at its genetic core, PepsiCo is not built for introducing healthy snack products that might take years of organic growth before gaining significant market share.

Of course, big companies like PepsiCo do use their resources to invest in studying the future. But this is only one capacity. Eventually, they have to make choices about what to actually do with the information. Too often, this data is simply not acted upon—in part because of the company's organizational DNA.

The circumstances of simply being large don't necessarily overwhelm every company's attempt to act and think with more of a focus on the future. Many large tech companies, for example, are designed to invest in the future. This sort of coding is fundamental to surviving in an industry in which products become obsolete fairly quickly. In 2020, PepsiCo's top brand will be . . . Pepsi. That same year, Apple's top product will be . . . it's hard to say. It may be an iPhone. Or maybe a wearable. The only certainty is that it won't be the iPhone released two years earlier. PepsiCo introduces new products with the understanding that Pepsi will almost certainly be its number one brand in five years. Tech companies introduce new products to make the future.

Case study: Greyston bakes brownies to build a better future

Startups have a very different relationship to the future. Because they have little existing value, they are not backwards-looking. Instead of protecting and expanding market share of existing brands, they can be focused on innovation in one product at a time. This goes a step further than tech companies. Apple recovers after unveiling a failed gadget, whereas a startup might not get a second chance. For startups, their product launch *is* their future. But even if the importance of the future is at their genetic core, many small companies also face a conflicting circumstance. They may not have resources to look much beyond the "urgency of now."

Greyston Bakery in Yonkers, New York, makes lots of brownies every day. They have to, if they want to supply Ben & Jerry's ice cream with brownies for flavors like Chocolate Fudge Brownie. But the small company's long-standing relationship with a huge national brand isn't the most interesting thing about the bakery. Greyston is staffed through open hiring. There are no asterisks on that policy. Anyone can come in, sign up, and get called for a job as soon as one opens up. Previous work history, jail time, or other past events that might cost people work at most other companies don't matter at Greyston.

This is a huge step outside of normal values and, in fact, the bakery was founded by a Buddhist named Bernie Glassman. Glassman had spent time, by choice, living among the homeless of Yonkers. He decided to start a business to eradicate homelessness in the town. There were lots of services that people needed—healthcare, childcare, and jobs. Glassman wanted to offer jobs to the homeless of Yonkers, but his hiring policy is based on the Buddhist concept of opening doors to people who are suffering. In short, we aren't interested in what you've done; we're interested in what you can do. The bakery produces over 30,000 pounds of brownies every day that are carried at upscale stores like Whole Foods with a staff comprised of many people who wouldn't be hired anywhere else.

Somewhat ironically, the bakery, famous for its forward-looking hiring policy, has a hard time looking far beyond the next batch of brownies itself. The bakery, which is a for-profit, sends its profits to a non-profit foundation. The foundation's goals include efforts to eliminate homelessness in Yonkers, but also spreading its open hiring policy. But moving beyond the day-to-day operations to these greater missions is difficult. Mike Brady, Greyston CEO, said that "The organization comes at it a lot of different ways. Some elements of the organization come from a scarcity mentality—we only have so much funding and opportunity." Small mission-driven companies like Greyston Bakery are stretched thin and don't have the resources to look very far ahead. They don't have funding to create advanced metrics about the future. But Brady is determined to do just that with the resources he can drum up.

Developing integrative thinking

Often we assume that the business pursuit of profit has to be at the expense of creating products that benefit people and the environment. Or conversely, that companies with a positive mission cannot perform well financially. But future first companies that want to do good and do well at the same time must develop integrative thinking across their strategy, their teams, their organization structure, and their company's culture and DNA.

Case study: Apple's integration through product teams

Take, for example, Apple. There are perhaps a million theories about why the company has been so successful. Many people point to former CEO Steve Jobs' vision. This is not entirely accurate. Jobs' leadership is discussed in almost mythical terms—a dropout Buddhist genius, a maniacal perfectionist. But what made Apple work was much less personal. It was not the CEO himself, but how certain qualities of the company's leadership were captured in a specific DNA and pushed out into the company.

At its genetic core, Apple has an organizational structure that is very unusual for a company its size. The company's DNA created certain unique organizational capabilities. Unlike many other companies, Apple is aligned by functions, like marketing, hardware, and software. This structure enables the company's primary capability: producing innovative consumer products. People can come together from all different parts of the company and operate as an integrated team for an intense product development process. Teams are assembled from different functional groups to design, develop, and launch new products like the iPhone. Then they go back to their original functional group when the product cycle is complete.

The DNA of many other companies, including huge tech companies like Microsoft, creates a more siloed organization. The result is that while Microsoft has some strong capabilities, it has often struggled to consistently innovate like Apple. In 2013, Microsoft's CEO, Steve Baller, attempted to reorganize Microsoft away from separate product divisions to a functional structure like Apple. But it didn't fundamentally change Microsoft. This is primarily a result of the companies' different DNA. The leadership that drove Apple's continual innovation was not Steve Jobs walking around Cupertino in a black turtleneck, inspiring—or perhaps intimidating—people with his presence. Every successful leader or leadership team creates a DNA with certain organizational capabilities that they then push out into the organization.

Case study: The OpEd Project to get the best ideas heard

In early 2005, syndicated columnist Susan Estrich took then-editor of the *Los Angeles Times*, Michael Kinsley, to task for the dearth of women published in his newspaper's opinion pages. At the *Los Angeles Times*, and pretty much every other major news outlet, there was a huge gender imbalance in who wrote opinion pieces: Only about 15 percent of the authors were women.

Katie Orenstein, a journalist and activist, discovered that the solution to the underrepresentation of women in the opinion pages was hidden in plain sight. "People were addressing the issue in broad ideological ways, for example by asking is the problem a result of sexism, biology, or socialization?", said Orenstein in an interview. "But I had not seen anyone address the specific problem that submission ratios were dramatically skewed; in other words, that women were not submitting to key op-ed forums with anywhere near the frequency that men were."

Media attention on the lack of women writers published in major news outlets across the country led the *Washington Post* to do a five-month survey on the massive gender gap in authorship of opinion pieces. The study reiterated what Orenstein and other writers and editors knew already. The issue was not the percentage of women's opinion pieces being published, because the submission-to-publication rates in terms of gender were roughly equal. The problem was that most of total submissions to newspapers across the US came from men, which meant women were being published at much lower rates than men. Research showed that female authors also comprised less than 20 percent of total submissions to the *Los Angeles Times* and other papers, so the problem wasn't as much in the final selection process but in the number of women who were submitting.

Orenstein decided that there was a "radically pragmatic solution" to this specific problem of underrepresentation: More women had to submit material to opinion forums. "If you wanted to ask, 'Why are there no girls in fifth grade?' you would certainly make sure to ask, 'Well, are there any girls in fourth grade?' It's just that painfully obvious." For Orenstein, it was not much of a leap to figure out how to address the issue. But since no one else was directly addressing the specific problem of submission rates, Orenstein created a seminar program to show women (and some men) the craft of writing a convincing opinion piece by tapping into the power of their individual expertise and sense of social responsibility. Her program grew into The OpEd Project, a social enterprise dedicated to increasing the range of voices and quality of ideas heard in the world by offering an innovative blend of public and private programs.

The OpEd Project's public programs have a "sustainable social justice" scholarship policy, so that programs can be afforded by any underrepresented person who is committed to changing the world through their voice. The OpEd Project's highest impact program is their Public Voices Fellowship program, which they run nationwide in partnership with universities like Yale, Stanford, and Princeton, and foundations like the Ford Foundation. The Public Voices Fellowship program is designed for approximately twenty underrepresented thought leaders and lasts for at least one year, dramatically increasing the participants' opportunities to have a public voice.

Orenstein tells a story about one of their Public Voices fellows at Yale University, Zareena Grewel, submitting a piece to *The New York Times* in 2015 about a drone strike in Mosul that killed people in her family. Grewel was well aware that the US Pentagon was not acknowledging what happened until the *New York Times* called them up and said, "We're running this piece, do you have a comment?" And then the Pentagon was forced to acknowledge what really happened. That's a living example of the importance of having a public voice. As Orenstein said, "It's not just about our fellow. It's about her family in Mosul. A group of people who, historically, might not have had any voice or say, and might have died invisibly."

In the years since Orenstein started The OpEd Project, the representation of gender in national opinion pages, like the *New York Times* and the *Wall Street Journal*, has increased from 15 percent to more than 21 percent. The kind of success The OpEd Project has had grew out of refusing to simply engage in an ideological debate. Of course, founder Katie Orenstein was offended by assumptions that there were substantially fewer women's bylines being published due to a lack of ability. But instead of getting stuck in the ideological debate about this problem, she found a powerful and pragmatic solution.

Bringing broader values into business decisions

Business decisions have always been made from values that go beyond simple financial metrics, but these values are often implicit. When DuPont decided not to replace the PFOA in their products with a less toxic but more expensive alternative, they were putting immediate profit first and the ongoing health of their workers and local communities affected by the toxic runoff from their plants last. Future first companies make all the values that go into every business decision explicit, so they can make better decisions about the company and about building the broader and long-term value of the company.

Case study: Google's omnipresence

Google is known for its mission to digitize all human knowledge, driving cars, and, in governance circles, for its unusual stock structure. Starting back in 2004, the company initially offered two classes of stock. Class A shares had one vote per share while the other option, B shares, entitled the holder to ten votes. But the B class shares are still primarily held by Google co-founders Sergey Brin and Larry Page, meaning they cannot be outvoted by all other shareholders. The result of this structure is that Google can have a market capitalization in the hundreds of billions without its co-founders giving significant control to shareholders. They can have their cake and eat it too.

This governance relationship is, in one sense, extremely anti-democratic. Traditionally, shareholders are supposed to be owners of the company with a say in how it is managed. On the other hand, Google's 2004 IPO statement included its catch phrase "Don't Be Evil." This undemocratic stock structure provides a way to protect its values. The company sees its mission as greater than the standard profit maximization expected by shareholders. The co-founders have the freedom to invest huge amounts of money into moonshot research and development schemes while refusing to allow graphic ads to show up in search results. Google's DNA is growth- and future-focused, and that is underwritten and ensured by the governance structure.

This sort of structure works well when you are Google, one of the top performing stocks over the past ten years. A shareholder who bought in at around $54 is unlikely to complain about leadership twelve years later when the stock is trading at around $1000 per share. Brin and Page get to keep throwing huge—but undisclosed—amounts of money into automotive and biotech markets. Investors' stock keeps going up in value. Everyone is happy.[2] Facebook, another huge and successful tech company, has also limited shareholder activity because they claim to be long-term oriented while many shareholders are short-term.

Case study: Patagonia, Etsy, Badger, and Seventh Generation

Other companies have deployed various techniques to get the financing available through IPOs without giving up control to the new "owners." Since 2010, an increasing number of US companies have registered as Benefit Corporations. The outdoor gear company Patagonia and stainless steel container manufacturer Kleen Kanteen are some of the most high-profile. Essentially, a Benefit Corporation is a for-profit entity that includes positive impacts on society, workers, community, and environment along with profit as part of their prescribed obligations.

In other words, the companies have legally locked in their DNA—a greater sense of mission—into their founding document. Most of the Benefit Corporations are privately held but, for public companies, the status clearly shows that they should not be held to the exact same standards as traditional shareholder-held businesses. The typical requirement of corporate leadership in public corporations is profit maximization. For the leadership of a Benefit Corporation, regarding profit as more important than these other requirements would be a dereliction of duty.

Beginning in the late 1990s, an upstart basketball apparel company began moving into national chains like Foot Locker nationwide. AND1 was the brainchild of three Wharton Business School students, but the brand gained its reputation through t-shirts with trash talk slogans and a marketing plan that included a gritty video mix tape of a street baller nicknamed "Skip to my Lou." AND1 added shoes and became the most successful brand in the basketball sector after Nike, which had owned the category for decades. The company also followed socially responsible practices like relying on inspection of its Chinese manufacturing plants, paying above-market wages to its US workforce, and donating 5 percent of its profits to charity. Once the co-founders were bought out, they watched as the new owners ditched all the future first goals in favor of profit maximization. Rankled, the three owners parted ways before reforming to create B Lab, a non-profit group that offers certification for what they call B Corporations.

Today, Etsy, organic skin care company Badger, Seventh Generation eco cleaning products and hundreds of other companies have elected this designation. The idea behind a B Corporation is not particularly complicated, but it is not the same as a Benefit Corporation. A B Corporation is an entity that goes through a lengthy process to measure and, if necessary, improve its future first metrics. Though it is not a legally binding designation, B Lab claims that its certification process "bakes sustainability into the DNA of your company as it grows, brings in outside capital or plans succession." In other words, it creates space for a mission to survive new management, investors, or ownership.

Moving beyond one-company, one-leader

The traditional approach to developing leaders and businesses has been to focus on one leader at a time, whose job was to build a great company—with all the bells and whistles that entails. But companies that will build lasting future value have concluded that they cannot successfully achieve their mission with a one-company, one-leader approach anymore. More companies than ever are collaborating together in partnerships and coalitions on developing future first business practices, like using less toxic resources in their supply chain. They take an ecosystem approach by continuing to compete on differentiating factors like product design, while collaborating on less competitive factors, like the cost of certain materials.

Case study: the CEO Water Mandate

Big companies are banding together to manage resources like water, energy, and land. Take, for example, the CEO Water Mandate, which is endorsed by major companies, like Bayer, Coca-Cola, Dow Chemical, Heineken, and PepsiCo.[3] The mandate mobilizes business leaders to advance water stewardship, sanitation, and the Sustainable Development Goals—in partnership with the United Nations, governments, peers, civil society, and others. The mandate supports multi-stakeholder partnerships to address challenges related to water scarcity, water quality, water governance, and access to water and sanitation. Undoubtedly, corporate coalitions are a powerful way to gain control over material resources on which whole industries depend. Water is one of those resources that is harder to come by. So tools for collaboration over access to clean water will help to mitigate the risk of serious future conflicts over water between countries and companies.

Case study: the love child of Etsy.com

Etsy's first employee, Matt Stinchcomb, left the company in 2015. He now heads up Good Work Institute, a non-profit future first business school funded by, but otherwise separate from, the for-profit Etsy. "We're essentially saying, if we want to re-imagine how business is done, we need to re-imagine business education. The possible trajectories of the transformational business school are far apart," said Stinchcomb. The school could easily end up being a vanity project for successful executives—or the company's most important contribution to Stinchcomb's broader ideals: changing the consciousness of for-profit business.

Because his initial business training happened at a small screen-printing business, a rock band, and an upstart crafts website, Stinchcomb is very comfortable using a lot of language outside the normal management vocabulary. Now, with over a decade of business experience, he could certainly have adapted more of the contemporary corporate cant. Instead he talks passionately about, for example, "the disconnection that we're feeling from ourselves, from one another, from the natural systems in the world—more suicide, more war, more extremism. Read any paper and you know what's going on." It's clear that his use of the language is intentional. "I want to bring wisdom to business. I want to have that conversation around fear, and spirituality, and death, and all of these things, because I feel like these are topics that aren't typically brought up in business."

He is also likely to go after accepted corporate concepts that would seem more aligned with his vision. For example, he sees "sustainability" not as a great goal to strive for, but a "less sad" marker to be moved past. In his words:

> A lot of businesses will push "30% less packaging." It's better, but it's still not good. We're not going to 30% less package ourselves out of climate change. We have to shift our attention beyond sustainability: We don't want to sustain the world that we've created right now.

It's hard to argue when Stinchcomb described our economy as one "that's created so much inequality. The way I look at it is that business is a tool. That tool is very powerful." Whether this kind of idealism will make a dent in the larger for-profit world is a moot point for Stinchcomb. He is focused on designing a new kind of business education.

Aside from promoting exposure to different language and value systems, Good Work Institute has three primary missions, targeted for customized interpretation of their curriculum. The first is to partner with a wide variety of organizations in the New York area, including universities and community centers, like the 92nd St YMCA, as well as local businesses, like Greyston Bakery.

With these projects, Stinchcomb is targeting what he calls "going deep"—creating a huge number of businesses as opposed to scaling up a smaller number of companies.

> The idea for change is really about empowering a big number of small local businesses, rather than trying to add the next Facebook, or some next big software company. If a community needs a cooperative grocery store and it employs five people, that's a huge success. We just want to do that a million times.

Stinchcomb's second project is an "immersive program," a kind of six-month business education program that brings "entrepreneurs, financial backers, mentors, all together through an implementation of the curriculum, and then they actually co-develop businesses that are needed by specific communities in the Hudson Valley." The program was piloted in 2015 and is now running the fourth annual program in 2018.

Finally, the curriculum that is developed and tested locally will be released as a free online version. "We would let anyone who wants to create their own business school do it free, and give them all of the resources that they need to run their own mini-regenerative business school." The Good Work Institute currently shares their reading and curriculum online.

The open-source curriculum which can create change by spreading virally through a large number of companies speaks to one of Stinchcomb's biggest goals. When describing Etsy's original runaway success, Stinchcomb speaks in the language of someone who respects the importance of ecosystems—the need to eliminate the worship of short-term, singular success. "We have to change the full conversation of what success means, and what success looks like. Unfortunately, we have a culture now that glorifies heroes of business—these 22-year-old tech entrepreneurs who became billionaires in a week."

Why future first DNA matters more than ever

Etsy has had a fascinating ride over the past twelve years, from a surprisingly successful craft website to an ungainly organizational mess to a publicly held B Corporation that combines rigorous metrics complemented with its original values. But what does this story mean for the future? And how much of its successes and failures are applicable to other businesses?

Traditional metrics of business success are mixed. Etsy still does a huge volume of business, but as of January 2018 the stock was worth about 70 percent of its opening valuation in April 2015. It's possible that Etsy will achieve founder

Kalin's original vision of building a company for the next one hundred years. But given the fleeting nature of tech companies and the rapid transformations in manufacturing, it seems unlikely that the Etsy of 2028 will look much like the company of today.

Future first capabilities, like embracing innovation as a sustainability challenge, developing integrative thinking, overcoming presentism, expanding the value of business decisions, and moving beyond one-leader and one-company, are what companies of all sizes and stages of growth need to develop. The story of Etsy discovering their mission and values retrospectively and by trial and error is what many startups run by creatives do. But it's never too early in a company's lifecycle to plan to build capabilities that will future-proof the company for growth through the inevitable storms of change and uncertainty ahead. And it is never too late for leaders of large companies to invest in reinventing their companies' capabilities to create the innovative products, people, and processes that can deliver generations of lasting future value.

Notes

1 Gold, M. (2003, January 12). Docket # 02P-0317 Recall Aspartame as a Neurotoxic Drug: File #4: Reported Aspartame Toxicity Reactions. *FDA Dockets Submittal*. Retrieved from www.fda.gov/ohrms/dockets/dailys/03/jan03/012203/02p-0317_emc-000199.txt
2 Chasen, E. (2015, August 12). Google's multi-class stock structure made alphabet move unique. *The Wall Street Journal*. Retrieved from http://blogs.wsj.com/cfo/2015/08/12/googles-multi-class-stock-structure-made-alphabet-move-unique/
3 Endorsing companies. (2017). Retrieved from http://ceowatermandate.org/

7   The value of future first talent strategies

In the summer of 2014, a group of leading tech companies released diversity data on their employees. The numbers were unimpressive, if largely expected. For one, the gender gap was dismal. Among fifteen of the largest companies who released data, only about three out of ten employees were women. The combined percentage of African-American and Hispanic employees at Google, Yahoo, Facebook, and LinkedIn averaged about 6 percent of the companies' total workforces. The representation of white women and people of color in leadership positions was even lower.

Most companies accompanied their data with statements expressing dissatisfaction and commitment to do better. But the truth is that, for all their innovation in other realms, companies like Twitter, Facebook, Apple, and Cisco have largely failed at creating employees that look like the country—or their customers. Worse, these companies are based in diverse California, the first US state in which non-Hispanic whites no longer comprise the majority.

While the tech companies' self-reporting was panned in the media, the industry is far from the least inclusive. The same tendency pervades in most economically and socially powerful industries, which is predominately hiring white males into leadership positions in even more concentrated numbers. Financial services managers, for example, are 81 percent white,[1] as are lawyers.[2] The gender gap is even worse in top corporations. In 2016, the percentage of female CEOs in Fortune 500 companies was a mere 4 percent and even fewer Fortune 500 CEOs are people of color.[3]

Women of all races are underrepresented in the most powerful industries, such as business, technology, finance, science, and law, but are overrepresented in "pink collar" industries, like education and childcare. The most diverse industries—health, hotel, catering, and service—also tend to offer positions with substantially less economic and social power. And even in these lower-status industries, white males sit disproportionately in the top leadership positions, which have more status and better pay.

It is practically impossible to find a company today that doesn't at least pay some lip service to diversity and what is now often referred to more broadly as inclusivity. So why are the most powerful leadership roles and jobs in the most lucrative and authoritative industries still predominately held by white men? And how does the overrepresentation of white men in the most lucrative positions in the economy contribute to wealth and income inequality?

This problem is so pernicious in large part because of our institutionalized and often unconsciously held views of who is most valuable and most entitled to hold economic and social power. We unconsciously accept the belief that it's safer to hire people into powerful roles who look and act just like those who have historically been in power and are still in power today. This dynamic, which determines who gets hired or invested in, virtually always works in favor of straight, white males. Ultimately, it also drives discrimination in hiring decisions—not only women and men of color, but also millennials and younger and older people, immigrants, LGBTQ people, and even the previously incarcerated or homeless.

The other part of the problem of the overrepresentation of white males in the most powerful roles and industries, is that work in the most lucrative and authoritative industries is often designed around traditional gender roles and family structures. It is simply hard to make partner, except for a small few, in a private equity firm, a law firm, or a consulting firm, where the partner track has been designed with the assumption of a spouse who stays at home, works part-time, or works full-time and still performs a second shift, to take care of the kids and home. For non-traditional families, in which a working parent is single or their partner works full-time, or their partner expects to equally share in the unpaid workload of taking care of children and the home, the partner track becomes far more elusive. It is typically a white male power elite that has the luxury and status of a spouse who performs most of the unpaid and lower status work to keep up the family and home, which replicates an old power economy from one generation to the next. It also contributes to the growing income and wealth gap in the US.

In other words, the fact that so many companies and industries still fail to achieve their goals for inclusively hiring and promoting talent cannot be explained with a one-dimensional story about diversity numbers. Neither can it simply be fixed with better recruiting or hiring practices. Many companies have hiring managers who unconsciously prefer to repeat their past hiring decisions, rather than focusing on and embracing a more diverse leadership and talent pool for the future. They either hire people who look like them or like the other people who already work at and hold positions of power in the company. Because the less diverse past and present informs our decision-making processes, it can be hard for managers to imagine and therefore recruit, hire, and promote white women and people of color into powerful roles across many industries. Because the career paths to get to the top of the house in financial services, law, government, science, and business have been historically designed with the assumption of traditional gender roles and families, it can be a real challenge to get top decision-makers to rethink the career paths (and the traditional gender and family models) that got them to the top of their fields.

This self-perpetuating dynamic is dangerous. It ignores the tidal wave of shifting demographics and power dynamics across countries, cultures, and business ecosystems around the world. By 2050, the US population and labor pool will be majority non-white. Today, young women are graduating from college and graduate school in greater numbers than their male counterparts. Companies must develop the capacity to look toward that future in their hiring practices and decisions.

The current backward-facing institutional mindset and old power economy cannot be fixed with a simple quota for race and gender diversity numbers and then ticking a box when it is met. Yes, there should be metrics that encourage business leaders to go beyond hiring people who don't necessarily sound, look, or act just like them. But this numbers game is ultimately a shallow kind of diversity that is not much more of a game changer than the tokenism of hiring one white woman or person of color on a corporate board.

Future first business leaders go beyond the one-dimensional view of diversity as a shallow, even cosmetic, effort by digging deeper into the meaning and value of building diverse leaders and teams for their companies. They understand how to seed and develop a broad set of strategies to empower their talent from pipeline to promotion, both for business value today and down the road. And they have a new power economy in mind when they design the career paths to the top of the organization that make economic and social power more accessible to men of color, women, and non-traditional families.

More than ever, future first leaders need to know how to recognize and bring out talent in high-performing and high-potential candidates who don't necessarily fit the old job mold. Leaders need to look more broadly for who will be in their talent pool, who is ascending the ladder of economic and social power, what matters most to them, and how to personally relate to and empower them. Future first business leaders who understand how to build and empower inclusive leaders and teams will have a huge leg up on the common global challenge of social dynamism.

One of the central challenges of truly investing in the next generation of talent is that leaders must reexamine the workplace values they take for granted. The next generation of talent, for example, might care more than you do about work-life balance, temporal flexibility, personal authenticity, social equality, or a sense of meaning and purpose at work. The future of your company's talent depends on your ability to understand what others value most and strategically reinvent your company's culture to uphold the most critical of these values.

Business leaders around the world, from technology companies to private equity firms to science departments, are seeing the writing on the wall that without future first talent strategies, they will not have the solid talent pipeline to succeed beyond the 2020s. They are asking how they can build business cultures that attract, select, and promote white women, people of color, immigrants, and millennials in greater numbers than they do today. Future first talent and hiring practices lock greater impact and value into the company's future.

Future first leadership as the bedrock of talent strategies

Future first organizations require power and authority to be more distributed throughout a network of relationships. For distributed networks to succeed, leaders must develop the interpersonal skills and multicultural competence to be effective with future first talent and teams. Future first leaders cannot afford to be walled off in a powerful organizational hierarchy anymore, where they don't know how to read and respond effectively to the social cues of those with less power.

Another trend that future first leaders are aware of and which they work with is that as customers and employees get less white and male, they are having trouble relating to and trusting leadership that is comprised mostly of white males. This is why committing to inclusive talent now is so critical. Future first companies won't be the ones having to scramble to tap into the future talent pool, particularly when the company's executives are ready to retire. The demographics are already changing dramatically.

To compete for talent both now and down the road, leaders have to be comfortable overcoming implicit biases in job descriptions, and in the recruiting and hiring processes as well as in developing people. Future first talent strategies must be built on a strong foundation of leadership, which can come from partnership and an integrative mindset. The future belongs to companies that can attract, retain, and develop future first talent by distributing power across a richly diverse talent pool.

Overcoming power blindness as a relational leader

"You know what I want to hear?" said Chad Pomeroy, a mission-driven white male executive. "I want to hear a personal story." Today, leadership is more and more about personal relatability. For Pomeroy, who has worked in executive positions in publishing, financial services, and now healthcare, a personal story offers authenticity.

> Whenever I hear an executive, or a CEO, or somebody who's looking at change and facing change—if I hear them talk about why it resonates for them as an individual, and a story that matters, I believe them a hundred times more than someone who just says, "Hey, we want to be an innovator. We want to be first at something."

Pomeroy is a leader who tries to walk his talk about authentic and personally related leadership. Today Pomeroy is Chief Solutions and Technology Officer at Evolent Health.

Evolent's innovation is to reimagine the way healthcare is delivered by creating provider-driven models. "Being in a race and being passionate are two different things. So I look for a story, I look for a personal connection." That personal connection and relatedness is expected to go both ways. With the lowering of boundaries between employees' personal and professional lives, people want leaders with whom they can have a two-way relationship.

While there are good reasons for this direction of more personally related leadership, it can conflict with developing inclusive talent strategies. Behavioral and social scientists have found that people in positions of power tend to ignore the social cues of people with less power than them.[4] Social cues can be verbal. But they can also be non-verbal, like facial expressions, body language and posture, and gestures. Power-blind leaders miss valuable information about how their employees are actually responding to them, and so they can be perceived as hard to relate to and remote. But future first leaders overcome the tendency to pay too little heed to their junior employees and to people from diverse groups they may implicitly assume are less powerful.

Future first leadership through partnership

Kirsten Tobey, who we met in Chapter 3, attributes a lot of the success of Revolution Foods to the relationship that she and Richmond (née Groos) developed early on. Every business needs strong and aligned leadership, but Tobey describes their bond as a different level of commitment. "We looked across the table at each other," said Tobey. "We got into this together and we're going to stick through, and it will be like a marriage."

The company's slogan is "Moms on a Mission," and the cooperative leadership style Tobey describes certainly sounds more like that of married parents than a traditional corporate model. Tobey said they had a firm understanding at the beginning about roles: "Kristin is an amazing CEO and team leader; I did more of the internal work around our operational model and our nutritional model and our HR." The alignment allowed both women to operate at their highest level. "We've crafted our roles in a way that capitalizes on our strength and balances our weaknesses with each other," said Tobey. "That's made for a really strong partnership."

But their relationship has always had important flexibility. Families, for example, add a certain amount of additional work and unanticipated factors into the equation. Since both women are moms, they knew that they needed to be able to cover for each other. Just as spouses may have to switch roles temporarily, Tobey and Richmond can take over the other's role when necessary. Tobey describes this attribute as having "mobility." Their partnership builds redundancy into their leadership roles, which allows them to be ready for the unexpected in their professional and personal lives.

This is not to say that they don't have disagreements, just that they handle them respectfully. "In parenting, you don't disagree in front of your kids. We don't disagree about things in front of our team. We work it out as friends."

Many successful leaders of social impact companies have discovered the power of partnership. Opower was co-founded by partners, Alex Laskey and Dan Yates. When Alex described the beginning of their partnership to me in an interview, he said:

> My close and long-time friend, Dan Yates, approached me and said, "We ought to do something together to have a positive impact on the environment. You care about this. I am now impassioned about this as well. And I think we'd make a good team." He came to me at a time when I was ready

to consider what I wanted to do next. I respect him, so we started exploring different ideas together. But all of them were first and foremost with a social mission.

Digging deeper to hire future first talent

Alex Laskey confided in me in an interview for this book that after years of successfully scaling Opower, the company he founded with Dan Yates:

> It came to our attention that we had ended up with a much less diverse employee base than we wanted. And we changed. In the last eighteen months, the company started implementing a bunch of unconscious bias training for everybody, and we went through our hiring practices to change job descriptions, and change the way interviews were conducted.

Laskey and Yates are future first leaders who built a very successful company with a critical environmental mission. But even they were not immune to the tendency to hire and invest in people from demographic groups that have (or who have historically had) the most economic and social power. The big difference is that once Laskey and Yates became aware of the limited diversity in their company, they brought their mission-driven leadership to solving the problem.

When I asked Alex how they had developed their hiring practices to grow Opower, he told me:

> One of our early advisors was a guy named Hadi Partovi who's been a very successful serial entrepreneur and investor. He was for a long time the only official advisor to Facebook. He was on the board of and an early advisor to Dropbox. He helped found Tellme, which was sold to Microsoft. Basically, one of the things he said which resonated with us and remained a kind of mantra was that, "A players hire other A players, B players hire C players."

Yet even using the most rigorous hiring processes that assess for job role "fit," the unconscious biases of the assessor about what a high performer in a high-status executive role looks and acts like creep into their judgment of what constitutes a "good fit." And the assessor has to carefully distinguish between the competencies for the role that the person could likely develop and the competencies that are likely immutable. Who is considered by default to be the "best fit" for these powerful jobs? Often the catch is that hiring the most obvious fit for the job seems like the lowest-risk hiring decision in the short term. But in the long run, hiring the same leadership profile, often white and male, because that seems like the safer bet can jeopardize the long-term value that could can come with developing a more inclusive talent pool.

Future first companies that are starting out will often fall back on less diligent hiring practices based on the "gut feeling" of leaders or a very superficial job interview. Younger candidates have less of a proven track record to assess and require even more of a judgment call about their future performance. Newer companies have less well-defined roles, and they may plan to keep it that way for years to come. It is even less obvious how to hire more objectively, and thus unconscious biases come into play, even in the most mission-driven business environments.

Behavioral scientists have found that a hiring manager can give non-verbal cues through their body language to an interviewee to signal whether the person is an in-group or out-group candidate. We know that it's hard for many hiring managers to imagine diverse candidates as a good fit for roles with power, despite their qualifications. Because such non-verbal cues operate unconsciously, a candidate from a group that is atypical for a particular role could actually perform worse in the interview. The same hidden dynamic can occur every day at work for people who are in the gender or racial minority or from other underrepresented groups, creating additional performance obstacles for them to overcome.

Hiring practices that give back to the local community

Nancy Pfund, founder of DBL Partners, who we met in Chapter 3, has developed and tested the investment thesis that any business can have a social impact through their hiring practices. She started in impact investing at Hambrecht and Quist (H&Q) as it was being acquired by Chase Bank, and the investment bank kept up their involvement with community funding in Oakland/Richmond and other low-income Bay Area neighborhoods, even after Chase bought H&Q in 2000 and then JPMorgan, where her first fund was hatched.

When Nancy spun out her own impact investment firm in 2008, DBL Investors, she continued to pursue companies that would make positive social impacts. DBL invested in The RealReal, which has its headquarters in a low-income neighborhood. The RealReal's warehouses provide quality job opportunities with quality benefits, according to founder and CEO Julie Wainwright, and "provide a place for autonomy and career advancement."

Pfund was also an earlier investor in SolarCity and Revolution Foods where, she said, "we worked really hard to hire diverse low-income employees." SolarCity, one of the nation's largest designers and installers of rooftop solar, has a diverse workforce that was 28 percent Latino at the time of the Tesla acquisition.

> We want to make companies look more like America. These are companies with jobs that are available to people who can't work in traditional tech companies like SolarCity and Tesla that offer great jobs to a diverse set of people, not just to those who already know how to code.

As an added benefit, their inclusive hiring practices helped companies like SolarCity build political credibility when they traveled to Washington, DC to build supportive policies, due to the fact that job creation is one of the holy grails of politics.

Quality job creation is also a more profound contribution to the community. Many companies make charitable contributions to local groups, like the Boys & Girls Club of America. This is useful in supporting good causes and organizations, but it is effort that's purely external to the company. By hiring a diverse workforce, companies are able to make something that is fundamental to their business success also become a contribution to the community.

Getting the most from future first talent

Social psychologists have been trying to figure out for decades what motivates people at work. What gets people to be more productive, creative, innovative, and collaborative on the job? It turns out that most people are motivated by a good fit between their strengths and values and what it takes to excel in their job and work culture. Future first leaders are able to custom-fit the right people into the right jobs and then empower and develop them to grow with the company.

Beyond the initial hiring process, there is a promotion and retention piece at play for future first employees. As it turns out, being a mission-driven company or having the company's core purpose be future first attracts and rewards talent. It can provide more intrinsic motivation as well as extrinsic motivation.

Inclusivity of all kinds leads to better retention of employees from under-represented groups as well as more creative problem solving and innovation. Women who work in an environment with few to no female colleagues, mentors, or managers are much more likely to leave the company than those in companies with more women. This highlights the fact that if you don't get your company to a healthy level of inclusivity, you are more likely to lose even those diverse employees you do hire, increasing turnover costs and losing competitive talent.

Inclusivity not only requires companies to adopt the most important values of employees into their workplace culture; it also allows many companies to meet the values and expectations of their customers. More diverse companies effectively reach a larger number of consumers from different backgrounds or communities. This is particularly true in an increasingly globalized world.

Developing future first teams through mentorship

Jeanna Kimbré, who we met in Chapter 4, is an industrial designer who has worked at large companies and startups across Asia and Europe. Today she lives in Tokyo and heads up Studio Five, one of Sony's design studios, as well as Studio Nordic in Sweden. Her team works on everything from UX research, UI color, and material design and packaging for Sony's products to images for marketing. She has seen firsthand the struggles of large companies to hire for gender and diversity.

"I think most leaders go for people who are similar to them because that's the easiest to manage," said Kimbré. She has assembled a highly diverse team and sometimes pays the price. "My management team and art director team drive me to the edge sometimes, because I have to communicate the same message in five different ways for all of them to be able to absorb it." But the pay-off is worth it. While she sees diversity as a worthy goal in itself, it also has clear functional advantages:

> Yes, it's quite hard to drive a team that's that diverse, but they push me to always think new. They challenge me all the time, and I think as a manager whether it's in a small corporation or a big corporation that's super important. I have eight super different angles on the same either issue or something that's going on in the company.

The result is innovation. Additionally, according to Kimbré, future first teams are more robust:

> Big companies go through big working crises and profit losses all the time … And I think what I really come to realize as a manager is that the more diverse my team is, the more chance I have in a time of crisis or if I need to innovate something to really kind of push and pull and come up with new things.

Building up gender diversity in Japan was a unique challenge. In Japan, Kimbré learned that while many women are employed, they generally stop working once they have children. As another metric, the Japanese Diet—the national legislature— is less than 10 percent women.[5] Additionally, Japanese organizational culture is traditionally much more hierarchical than the flatter, more open managerial style that Jeanna practiced. Fortunately, Kimbré's boss, a man, made it clear that she wasn't supposed to learn how to think and act Japanese. Instead, he encouraged her to be a catalyst for new thinking, including being a mentor for Japanese women working with her at Sony.

Advancing and retaining future first talent

Co-founder of Opower, Alex Laskey, said:

> What we discovered [was] that our real problem was not in hiring, but in internal promotion. We hired a ton of women at junior levels and it wasn't that they weren't promoted as quickly. But we started prioritizing, in the last 18 months, developing high-potential employees—both men and women. It's having the effect of helping accelerate the development for women.

Where women are concerned, future first leaders need to be mindful of the value of creating a working environment that treats women as equals but doesn't necessarily expect everyone to be motivated by the same things or to act in the same way.

Future first companies have better employee retention

Alex Laskey shared that one of their biggest success factors has been hiring and hanging on to top talent. Being a successful future first company went a long way toward retaining great employees:

> We hired away a lot of employees out of Facebook and Google and Amazon and other places. And we've kept those employees and kept other employees like them for a long, long time, because they're proud of the company that they worked for.

Co-founder of Revolution Foods, Kirsten Tobey, shared in an interview that they have had success with employee retention and developing and promoting people. She said:

> Seeing employees develop with us is one of the most gratifying things for Kristin and me that we really didn't anticipate before we started. We have just gotten to the point in a couple of our regions where we have people celebrating their five-year anniversaries. Many of them started out as temp hourly employees and most of them have been promoted now to supervisory and manager positions.

It is not surprising that Revolution Foods has hung on to many of their employees. The company is very intentional about translating five core values into what they mean for employees. The core values form a two-way commitment between the company's leaders and employees. In Tobey's words:

> We make certain promises to the company based on those core values. And then what does it mean for the company—the company makes promises to its employees around those core values. So that I think it drives a lot of our employment practices. We generally really try to make sure that employees at all levels of the organizations feel ownership over the work that they are doing.

All employees at Revolution Foods, including the full-time hourly workforce, have stock options.

Ingersoll Rand, the global industrial products company, has an annual employment survey. The survey has a high rate of participation, although it is not mandatory. One of the highest-ranked areas of engagement among the company's tens of thousands of employees around the world is sustainability. "That lets us know that employees actually believe that we're on the right path," said Scott Tew, Executive Director at the company's Center for Energy Efficiency and Sustainability. "They believe that leaders that are in charge of the company strategy are serious about it." Not only that, but since the sustainability questions were added to the survey about four years ago, its employee importance has gone up every year.

Ingersoll Rand has huge opportunities for positive material impact with its energy-intensive products like air conditioners and transport refrigeration. For Scott, the work at his center has three impacts. One is the customer outcome, for example automation systems that lower a client's electricity usage. The second is efficiency and effectiveness in operations.

But the third impact relates to what Scott sees in the survey. "We think that sustainability also, like at many other companies, is a way to retain your employees." Not only that, but sustainability helps attract new, younger employees who perhaps have an expanded set of expectations for the company. "They just expect that we act a certain way," said Scott. "They expect more. And I think that's okay. And I think sustainability and our work around sustainability helps them know that their values are aligned with the company and that's what they want."

Purpose-driven brands appeal to your customers and employees

In 2004, the fifty-year-old Dove soap and personal care brand organized a show called "Beyond Compare: Women Photographers on Real Beauty" in a gallery space in Toronto. The exhibition included photos by dozens of female photographers, including famous names like Annie Leibovitz, Tierney Gearon, and Peggy Sirota. But it was the women in the photographs who were the emphasis. The subjects were not models or celebrities. They were specifically selected for their "ordinariness." By basing a high-profile show around these subjects, Dove hoped to start a broader discussion about how women feel about beauty.

The exhibition was also the first step in an incredibly successful global marketing initiative called the Dove Campaign for Real Beauty. Over the past thirteen years, the campaign has included print ads, hashtags, and selfie campaigns focused on "average bodies." A viral video called Real Beauty Sketches became the most watched video ad of all time. The campaign's success at recasting Dove as more than just a personal care product also sold lots of soap.

Recently, Dove put what was deemed to be a racist advertisement on Facebook, showing a black woman turning into a white woman when she took off her shirt. The implication was that Dove soap would transform a black woman into the ideal standard of beauty represented by a white woman. The good news was that because of Dove's reputation as a purpose-driven brand, they were immediately taken to task online for the racist message of the ad, and Dove apologized and removed the ad from Facebook.

In 2015, Dove's parent company, Unilever, announced that its purpose-driven brands such as Dove, Persil, Ben & Jerry's, Marmite, Pot Noodle, and Vaseline were growing twice as fast as other brands in its portfolio. Unilever labels these brands "sustainable living." Aside from being critical to the company's future plans for expanding sales, there is a less discussed impact of the fourteen to fifteen purpose-driven brands. As Unilever's VP of Corporate Sustainability put it, "The role of brands in society is changing to be more about what consumers need. When this happens, there is a snowball effect." Just as Dove attempted to forge a personal connection with girls and women by starting an open discussion about the impact of negative body image and negative self-images, the brand also forged a connection with its employees.

Employees working with Unilever's sustainable living brands tend to be more motivated by this positive relationship with the larger world. And the perception that they are making a difference by helping millions of girls think more positively about their body image also forges a more ongoing and authentic bond between the employees and Dove. The primary initiative of the Global Campaign for Real Beauty was to interest consumers in a novel way by acknowledging the fears and insecurities linked to self-image. Improving retention rates or imbuing employees with a greater sense of purpose was, at best, a secondary thought. But the campaign to publicize the potential negative impact of the beauty industry was also emotionally resonant with the values of employees.

Expand the value frontier with future first talent strategies

The argument that the US's diversity is its strength is commonplace, but it is not really leveraged by the country's overrepresentation of white males in the most powerful jobs and industries. Among the world's largest economies, the US is one of the most ethnically and linguistically diverse. This is a resource that should be used to reach new global markets by hiring employees who look more like the rest of the world.

Future first leaders seek to overcome the hidden power blindness that hamstrings traditional leaders by actively defining the value of their employees more broadly and inclusively. They view their role as leaders less in terms of their own power and more in terms of serving the development and empowerment of their employees. They distribute their power more broadly by giving it away, and in this way they create stronger networks of powerful relationships with and among their employees. They are open to listening and learning from their employees, which allows them to be more responsive and therefore more trusted.

When you give someone a job, you give that person economic power. When you also empower people, generally speaking, they will bring more of themselves to the workplace. Future first business leaders have the ability to hire and hang on to employees who don't look or act just like them, because that is often where the power of future talent lies.

Notes

1 Caldwell, P. (2014, March 11). The financial industry doesn't want you to know about its lack of diversity. *Mother Jones*. Retrieved from www.motherjones.com/politics/2014/03/financial-firm-diversity-jobs

2 Bourree, L. (2015, January 29). The least diverse jobs in America. *The Atlantic*. Retrieved from www.theatlantic.com/business/archive/2015/06/diversity-jobs-professions-america/396632/

3 Zarya, V. (2016, June 6). The percentage of female CEOs in the Fortune 500 drops to 4%. *Fortune*. http://fortune.com/2016/06/06/women-ceos-fortune-500-2016/

4 Fiske, S. (2011). *Envy up, scorn down: How status divides us*. New York: Russell Sage Foundation.
5 Editors (2016, May 12). Getting more women in the diet. *The Japan Times* Retrieved from www.japantimes.co.jp/opinion/2016/05/12/editorials/getting-women-diet/#.WAle8ztBzFs.

8 Multiplying your impact through ecosystem partnerships

Beyond developing leadership behaviors, beyond transformative hiring practices, beyond even the DNA of whole organizations, the greatest opportunity for change exists in business ecosystems. In fact, all these other aspects of future first leadership build up to the possibilities that exist beyond single leaders and companies. In this opening, businesses can both cooperate and compete, accelerating, multiplying, and scaling innovation. In short, business ecosystems are where the action happens now.

In a sense, the growing relevance of ecosystems has nothing to do with future first goals. Globalized companies have been more compelled to evolve away from operating as self-contained entities with one commander-in-chief at the helm than in previous decades. An ecosystem is broadly made up of networks of connections across multiple entities, large and small. Often the ecosystem network of one company spans many countries and regions of the world.

The growing importance of ecosystems has ushered in a new way of doing business, where traditional business taboos against teaming up with your competition no longer apply. Business leaders have more connections with other leaders and organizations within their ecosystem than ever before. Largely intermediated by technology, future first leaders have many opportunities to build partnerships across their business ecosystem to multiply their companies' impact.

This new environment also provides entirely new pathways for future first innovation. Through the ripple effect across a business ecosystem, small companies can have an outsized impact with a powerful innovation. When a new idea is distributed across the networks of an ecosystem, then a ripple effect multiplies the impact of that idea regardless of where it came from. Large companies can team up with other large companies or can bring in house the innovations of a small company in order to rapidly multiply their impact and the scale of those innovations.

This chapter highlights some of the most powerful types of future first partnerships that have had a multiplier effect across a business ecosystem. Many opportunities for partnership are available for future first leaders who want to accelerate their company's impact across their ecosystem. There are five future first partnership opportunities covered in the chapter: forming a David and Goliath partnership; expanding your mission with an acquisition; joining forces with your competition through an ecosystem coalition; paving the way for new government and consumer choices; and scaling up the alternative into something bigger and better. The partnership opportunities that would work best with your future first company depend on your company's ecosystem as well as its stage of growth and its scale.

The David and Goliath partnership

By their nature, business ecosystems do not have an up or down. They are non-hierarchical networks. Ideas and information move between different players who are linked in different ways. A larger player can adopt an innovation, forcing other smaller players to keep pace. But innovation often germinates in smaller players before being scaled up. Ecosystem networks facilitate the transfer of new ideas, knowledge, and products, which can happen in a flash or may gradually evolve over many years.

Cyril Gutsch, a German-born designer, had a revelation moment after meeting environmentalist Paul Watson. Shocked by Watson's description of the rapid die-off of coral reef in oceans, Gutsch converted his New York-based design company to an environmental organization called Parley and set about trying to make a difference. He settled on creating a yarn-like product out of ocean plastic that is fished out of the ocean and prepared for reuse. Then he partnered with Adidas, believing that the shoe company could be a player "who redefines the rules" in the apparel ecosystem. The first collaboration between Parley and the shoe giant is a running shoe upper sole made out of discarded plastic fishing nets that have been cleaned, ground, and woven into thread.[1]

Beyond the environmental imperative, Gutsch sees a clear competitive upside for Adidas and his other partners, which is investing in future-looking environmental processes and products. In the not-so-distant future, Gutsch believes that environmental degradation will lead to an enormous disruption in how we do business. When that happens, future first companies will have already converted their factories and have partnerships in place with forward-looking clients.

Halosource started out in 1999 as a small, scrappy pioneer in drinking water purification. Their breakthrough technology was a biopolymer hybrid that removes particulates from large volumes of water. Halosource patented the water purification technology as HaloPure and went public in 2010. Halosource is now a global company, based in the Seattle region, that has developed technology to bring safe drinking water to more than ten million people in China, India, and Latin America.

The company's CEO, Martin Coles, was formerly the President of Starbucks, and many members of the executive team have years of experience working in much bigger corporations. But Halosource is still a small company with an outsized impact due to their strategic partnerships with multinational corporations that sell their water filtration products in countries like India and China. For example, Halosource partnered with Tupperware to develop a water filter cartridge that fits a new line of Tupperware water filters first sold in India. In 2012, Halosource teamed up with China-based consumer product company, Perfect, to provide the water filter cartridge for Perfect's multi-stage water purifiers.[2]

Expanding your mission with an acquisition

In April 2000, Ben & Jerry's ice cream was bought by Anglo-Dutch multinational Unilever. It had all the makings of corporate culture disaster. Ben & Jerry's was well known for its quirky marketing campaigns, like the Cowmobile, in which the owners drove across the country dishing out free scoops. Unilever was primarily known for being the big and efficient parent company of Dove soap, Hellmann's mayonnaise, and thirteen other brands that each had over a billion dollars in annual sales. Ben & Jerry's Vermont headquarters were twenty-seven miles from the company's factory; Unilever was global with seven subsidiaries in major Asian markets. With all the differences, one of the biggest worries for Ben & Jerry's fans and employees was whether the company would stay committed to its social activism once Unilever came in with a mission to enforce fiscal discipline.[3]

The ice cream makers had a long history of political and charitable involvement. Starting in 1985, the Ben & Jerry's Foundation received 7.5 percent of annual pre-tax profits from the company to fund community-oriented projects. In 1988—the same year President Ronald Reagan named the founders as US small businessmen of the year—the company began buying brownies from Greyston Bakery, in part because of the bakery's progressive open hiring policy.

Unilever's first step incorporating Ben & Jerry's into its new parent company was naming French-born Yves Couette as CEO. Couette was a longtime corporate Unilever executive who had led businesses in Mexico and India. But he also realized the importance of maintaining his new company's market niche based on social activism and responsibility. He began by dressing down at work, but he also laid off hundreds of people and closed factories. Then he defended these bold moves—unprecedented in the company's twenty-two-year history—by saying that the best way to spread the company's unique business dynamic was by making it successful. Since then, his claim that he could grow profits while keeping the company's core values has been more true than not.

One example of how this partnership played out between a corporate giant and a mission-driven company is when Couette began using the Unilever performance management system at Ben & Jerry's; however, he adapted the system to include additional social performance metrics.

The left-leaning social activism has continued unabated. Ben & Jerry's was an early advocate for gay rights in the 1980s. In 2012, Ben & Jerry's changed the name of Oh! My! Apple Pie! to Apple-y Ever After to support equality for same-sex couples in the UK. To celebrate the 2015 legalizing of same-sex marriage in the US, they temporarily renamed Chocolate Chip Cookie Dough to I Dough, I Dough, with the proceeds going to a non-profit LGBT rights group.

A flurry of other progressive initiatives has continued at the iconic lefty company since the acquisition. Ben & Jerry's uses only cage-free eggs to make the ice cream. In 2013, the company committed to making GMO-free ice cream. In 2014, the company took the heat from Australian politicians after signing on to a group publicizing the destruction of the Great Barrier Reef from coral bleaching caused by warmer ocean temperatures. In 2015, the company partnered with Tesla to introduce a flavor called Save Our Swirled, to call attention to global warming and support climate talks in Paris. The company still gives around $1.1 million per year to charity. Its workers all make at least twice the national minimum wage. Its boldest role in recent years, however, was being the only corporation that publicly supported the Occupy Wall Street protestors in New York City.

All of this activism and social responsibility has continued despite the fact that the founders are no longer actively involved in the company's operations. This was made possible in part by a unique structure described in the sales agreement. An external board was created to make sure that Ben & Jerry's stayed true to its mission-driven goals. To avoid too much external interference, only two of the thirteen members can be appointed by Unilever. The board is involved in things like setting Ben & Jerry's livable wage policies. The company is now a B Corporation, providing additional metrics for sustainable business practices. At the same time, Ben & Jerry's revenues have tripled and it's been able to hire back more workers than were originally laid off.

While Ben & Jerry's has been able to retain much of its original social mission while scaling up, the real question is whether the company can continue to promote change over the long haul at its much larger parent company. To date, Unilever's focus has been to keep Ben & Jerry's true to its original values. In fact, Unilever's president of refreshments, Kevin Havelock, said his company has been impressed enough with Ben & Jerry's commitment and success to look at transforming Unilever itself into a B Corporation in the future.[4] If this were to happen, Unilever would be the first multinational corporation to become a B Corporation since the B impact standards first established a new type of socially responsible company in 2006. A bold move like this by Unilever would not just retain Ben & Jerry's mission, but promote it on a much larger platform. If successful, it would be a shining example for other corporations interested in adhering to progressive social and environmental standards while maintaining profitability. The tail may finally wag the dog.

Big food companies have an endless appetite for smaller brands that make local, organic, and socially responsible products. A number of other big food companies have bought up smaller, more innovative partners in response to the growing demand for organic food products in the US markets. Over the years, for example, Danone acquired Stonyfield Farm yogurt, General Mills bought Annie's Homegrown, and Campbell Soup swallowed up Plum Organics. Hormel bought Applegate Farms and the Kellogg Company purchased Kashi.

Many progressives take the default view that the small mission-driven company acquisition automatically spells a "sell-out." But Ben & Jerry's has demonstrated some very practical ways that this does not have to be the case. Business leaders of small future first companies can embrace partnerships with big companies as long as they maintain a certain amount of autonomy and control over their corporate culture and values. But it also means the horizons for transforming their ecosystem can be much broader and will take much longer.

Joining forces with your competition through an ecosystem coalition

The apparel industry has innumerable groups working to create industry cooperation toward more sustainable supply chain practices, with varying degrees of success. One of the better known, the Sustainable Apparel Coalition (SAC), was launched in 2009 by strange bedfellows, Patagonia and Walmart. Today the group includes dozens of retailers, manufacturers, and brands such as Nike and Eileen Fisher, as well as environmental partners like the National Resources Defense Council.

The coalition's most ambitious project has been developing the Higg Index. Named after the elusive Higgs Boson particle, the index is an attempt to create a measurement of the social and environmental impact of apparel across industries. SAC Executive Director Jason Kibbey described the creation of the index as a search for "the parts of the supply chain that would change sustainability."[5]

While developing the ability to track products across the complicated apparel global supply chain would be an enormous step forward in terms of data gathering, members are not bound to take any specific actions. Kibbey said that some coalition members have just "started to use the brand module or facilities module" while others are already "redesigning their sustainability programs around the use of the index."

Because so much apparel is made partly or entirely with cotton, another group, The Better Cotton Institute, is focusing on more sustainably growing the crop. The Better Cotton Institute brings together companies including World Wildlife Federation and IKEA to reduce the amount of chemicals and water used to raise cotton.

Cradle-to-Cradle Product Innovation Institute has created another certification for a wider range of products, from Method cleaner to Armstrong flooring adhesive and from shingle siding to body lotion. The institute was founded by environmental architect William McDonough and German chemist and former Greenpeace activist Michael Braungart. Its certification process grades products in five categories, including material health, material reutilization, carbon management, water stewardship, and social fairness.

Lewis Perkins, the director of the innovation institute, said the goal of the institute is to create a less wasteful, more circular economy. "Massive collaboration is what we're going to see both within industries and across industries within the circular economy," Perkins predicted. "We want our materials taken back, and companies will see an opportunity in doing this. Lots of collaboration can make it happen. One company can't solve it."[6]

The key to making the coalition partnership work is what Nike and Adidas have done with the apparel coalition. They cooperate on the features of the products and materials in their supply chain that are not competitive differentiators for them. So, if a particular fabric dye can be made more sustainably at a better price for the whole industry, it is more cost-effective for all the players. Nike and Adidas can still go head-to-head on product design while improving the environmental impact of their products.

Paving the way for new government and consumer choices

The buzz first began in the early 2000s. Walmart, a company synonymous with cheap plastic and low wages, was going green. The company had partnered with a group called the Carbon Disclosure Project to measure the greenhouse gases emitted by its operations. In 2007, the company extended the requirement to its enormous supply chain. More than 100,000 suppliers were supposed to measure their carbon emissions and environmental sustainability. A few years after putting these metrics into place, the giant retailer set goals. Between 2010 and 2015 it would knock twenty million metric tons of greenhouse gases off its supply chain. This is the equivalent of taking nearly four million cars off the road for a year.

To make sure the project moved ahead efficiently and had credibility, Walmart partnered with a range of organizations, including Environmental Defense Fund, PricewaterhouseCoopers, and a sustainability center at the University of Arkansas. The company could add solar panels to its rooftops or doors to its open refrigerator bins, but the bulk of the cuts were going to come from the manufacturing and shipping of the products that ended up on its vast shelves. This put the responsibility for change on their vast network of suppliers. This made sense, because the carbon footprint of the supply chain is much larger than even that of the enormous stores the company owned.

In addition to compelling other companies to look at their environmental sustainability, there was something bigger at work here. Walmart, as a private company, had the capacity to create massive change far ahead of what governments are able to impose. The Environmental Protection Agency (EPA) has had successes in regulating, for example, auto emissions for greenhouse gases. But there is virtually no chance the agency could suddenly demand Walmart impose the sorts of cuts it announced. As the second largest corporation in the world, Walmart has huge leverage with its suppliers, because most of them wouldn't dare risk losing the corporate giant's business. And yet, the results of these business-led measures were enormous. In 2005, the EPA had identified around two hundred model companies, labeled "climate leaders," that committed to a certain level of carbon cuts. Walmart's cuts were four times as big, and they saved the company millions of dollars in supply chain costs.

The company even tossed around the idea of a comprehensive sustainability index for products similar to the nutritional labels on food. Customers could see data in the supply chain all the way to producers—creating unprecedented transparency.

Since then, results have been mixed. Many critics claim that while Walmart has made splashy announcements about reductions, it is still one of the nation's largest and fastest-growing polluters. Walmart's shortcomings are at least partly due to the fact that the company makes money by shipping lots and lots of disposable stuff from factories on the other side of the planet. As such, Walmart's foray into carbon reduction remains more a model of the amazing possibilities of corporate social responsibility. The very fact that Walmart is still viewed by environmentalists as a dirty company actually makes this move powerful for the larger message it sends to other companies: Reducing carbon is good for your bottom line.

Since the middle of the twentieth century, chickens have been raised commercially on a steady diet of antibiotics. The drugs were an easy way for farmers to treat infections, but they were fed to all the animals regardless of whether they were ill or not. Some hormones were put in feed, not out of medical necessity, but to encourage more rapid growth. These techniques allowed companies to produce more chicken at lower prices, but there was a cost. The indiscriminate use of antibiotics began creating new diseases resistant to the drugs. Not only did this render some of the tools of veterinarians useless, some of the same diseases were making people sick.

An unlikely contender in the race to improve the quality of our food, McDonald's, announced in March 2015 that they would no longer sell chicken raised on antibiotics. A few days later, Costco Wholesale announced a similar policy. McDonald's was hardly the industry leader in this move—chains including Chipotle and Chik-Fil-A had already made the switch. Neither did the policy switch eliminate all chicken antibiotics or necessarily improve other conditions for chickens. The impact the decision did have was akin to Walmart's carbon reduction plan. It put huge pressure on the nation's largest chicken producer, Tyson, and other industry leaders who supply McDonald's with meat for their Chicken McNuggets. Tyson had to look at their feed supply differently. And they were suddenly playing catch-up with rival Purdue, a company that has been moving away from feeding human antibiotics to their chickens for over a decade and which in 2015 raised more than half of their chickens without ever feeding them antibiotics.

McDonald's and Walmart are hardly saving the world. They are not exactly future first companies yet. The negative environmental and nutritional impact of both businesses is enormous. Nonetheless, the raw power of their massive scale and profitability to act as global trendsetters makes a huge material difference. Walmart and McDonald's can set criteria, like reducing their carbon footprint or improving quality of food, across a massive supply chain. And, even without being mission-driven, they already see that they can do it without regulation imposed on them.

More than ever today, companies need to take a strong stand to get out ahead of government regulation and consumer choices, and set trends in products that are better for people and the environment. If Walmart and McDonald's are doing this in some areas of their business, then future first business leaders can certainly take even bolder steps to reduce carbon emissions and create quality products across their entire companies.

Scaling up the alternative into something bigger and better

Just as large companies can influence behavior across their supply chain, they can also influence another "external" factor: consumer demand. Whole Foods, recently bought by Amazon, is a classic example of a company that provided what a small number of consumers wanted—organic produce—but made it available on a large scale. The natural, organic, or local goods may have been available at farmers' markets or health food stores, but Whole Foods also created a different shopping environment—a full-sized, high-end supermarket versus the traditionally smaller, less slickly branded health food store.

Founded in 1980, Whole Foods expanded throughout the 1990s to become the nation's largest high-end supermarket focused on healthy, natural, and organic food and lifestyle products. Over the past twenty-five years, organic food and lifestyle products have also experienced an unprecedented 3,400 percent increase in sales. There is not a one-to-one correlation between Whole Foods' growth and the runaway success of organics. For example, much of Whole Foods' growth was a result of acquiring other companies with similar business models that also sold organics. The chain put innumerable smaller, traditional stores that would have been selling healthy foods out of business. But Whole Foods' high-end consumer experience put hormone-free sausage and organic red lettuce in front of tens of thousands of new customers. The end result is that thousands fewer agricultural workers were exposed to the pesticides used to make conventional agricultural goods.

Whole Foods' impact can be measured in a number of ways. First is growth so rapid that companies are paying their suppliers to switch to organic growing methods years before they will be able to produce anything labeled organic.

Second are products, like Campbell's organic chicken soup and Capri Sun Organic juice. Even the biggest food companies, known for their processed foods for decades, want to get a piece of the growing organic food market. Would the Fortune 500 food giants have wanted to get into organics without envisioning them on Whole Foods's shelves?

Maybe the best way to measure Whole Foods' impact is to look at how the chain has become a victim of its own success. Retail giants that had absolutely no interest in organics twenty-five years ago have committed heavily enough in the category that Whole Foods is no longer grabbing as much of that rapid rise in demand for organics. During the 2000s, when the bigger players largely ignored organic foods, the company's average growth was around 20 percent. Now it is below 4 percent as companies like Kroger and WalMart grab market share.[7] But this does not need to stop a future first player, like Whole Foods, from searching for the next value frontier in healthy food and lifestyle products.

Surprising elements of ecosystem partnerships

All of these future first partnerships have surprising and unlikely features. Who would have thought an environmentally progressive startup called Parley would convince Adidas to use recycled ocean plastics in their shoes? Few people expected that Ben & Jerry's would be able to hold firm on their progressive business values after getting acquired by corporate giant Unilever, let alone that they might even become the tail wagging the dog.

Many industries, like apparel, have formed ecosystem coalitions to leverage the scale of the corporate giants across an industry without compromising critical competition on product design and innovation. Some of the biggest corporate giants, like Walmart and McDonald's, are wielding the power of their massive size and reach to exert a positive impact and to set an example of what other huge corporate giants can do to get ahead of government regulation and consumer demand. Finally, though Whole Foods has been losing market share to big box grocery stores like Target and Walmart, their scale and reach will likely grow through Amazon's vast infrastructure of online retail. Whole Foods is a powerful example that future first companies can keep being pioneers by searching for what the healthy food shopping experience will look and taste like on the next horizon of their ecosystem.

Notes

1 Rhodes, M. (2016, June 7). Adidas spins plastic from the ocean into awesome kicks. *Wired*. Retrieved from www.wired.com/2016/06/adidass-newest-shoe-made-recycled-ocean-plastic/

2 Business Wire (2012, April 17). HaloSource signs first strategic Chinese partner. Retrieved from www.businesswire.com/news/home/20120417005739/en/HaloSource-Signs-Strategic-Chinese-Partner

3 Gelles, D. (2012, August 21). How the social mission of Ben & Jerry's survived being gobbled up. *The New York Times*. Retrieved from www.nytimes.com/2015/08/23/business/how-ben-jerrys-social-mission-survived-being-gobbled-up.html

4 Confino, Jo. (2015, January 23). Will Unilever become the world's largest publicly traded B corp? *The Guardian*. Retrieved from www.theguardian.com/sustainable-business/2015/jan/23/benefit-corporations-bcorps-business-social-responsibility

5 Godelnik, R. (2012, July 27). Interview: New tool will measure sustainability across apparel supply chains. *Triple Pundit*. Retrieved from www.triplepundit.com/2012/07/interview-sustainable-apparel-coalitions-executive-director-new-higg-index/

6 Lozanova, S. (2016, June 30). From pipedream to product innovation: The rise of the circular economy. *Triple Pundit*. Retrieved from www.triplepundit.com/special/defining-thought-leadership/thought-leadership-circular-economy/

7 Gensler, L. (2015, February 11) Whole Foods reports strong sales growth, expansion into Canada. *Forbes*. Retrieved from www.forbes.com/sites/laurengensler/2015/02/11/whole-foods-reports-strong-sales-growth-expansion-into-canada/#16d8fedb4d0d

Epilogue
Future first in the era of backwards politics

While I was writing this book, the US entered a new political era. In fact, combined with the UK's vote to leave the European Union and the strength of various right-wing populist candidates on the continent, there was a broader political shift around the world. On the surface, these changes manifested themselves in ways that directly contradicted future first goals. In the US, the reality of climate change was outright denied by the head of the federal agency responsible for protecting the country's environment. Trump's withdrawal of the US from the Paris Agreement was a big step backwards on a global climate change mitigation plan that many believe was not aggressive enough. There was a notable shift in political attitude, language, and even official policy that rebuked the values of diversity and inclusivity—be it socio-economic, racial, ethnic, gender, or sexual orientation. Perhaps even more striking was the retreat from the unavoidable consequences of social dynamism and engagement in a globalized world.

My book and the new political rhetoric both seek to change entrenched practices but, usually, in completely opposite directions. Future first leadership seeks to accelerate and scale the many already existing progressive elements found in private industry. America First seeks to use the federal government to tear down the present in favor of a boxed-in, retrograde vision of the future.

Fortunately, all of these seismic transformations in what I assumed the political terrain would look like in 2017 don't change the basic proposal of my book. If anything, they make innovating around global challenges even more urgent. The earth doesn't change on the basis of a single election; it will continue to heat up, with accompanying disruptions in weather patterns, crop production cycles, animal migration, and natural ecosystems all over the world. Resource scarcity, from water to platinum, will accelerate and change how certain industries operate. Likewise, the populations, workforce, and market opportunities in the US and Europe will grow less white. The presence and importance of women, men of color, and LGBTQ people in the workforce will increase. No matter who sits in the White House, the future still belongs to companies that innovate around these global challenges.

This is not to underplay the threat posed by politics that seeks to encourage the worst elements of traditional business practices—like exploiting short-term profits from reduced environmental regulation over toxins like PFOA that are well-known to be carcinogenic. There is a tangible value in the efforts of governments like Germany, which is closing in on its ambitious goal of getting 45 percent of its energy from renewable sources by 2030. In the US, the sort of public-private partnerships that have helped drive down the price of batteries by 75 percent over the last eight years are at risk.

But the truth is that regardless of the administration, governments are typically laggards when it comes to addressing future first global challenges. Based on their current trajectories, for example, government initiatives aren't going to produce anywhere near the rate of change needed to meet the very real needs of a hotter, more crowded planet. But while administrations on the right and left have come and gone, the power of the private sector has grown and consolidated massively over the past forty years. For better or worse, business has become the most powerful force of change on the planet. When governments step back from incentivizing the development of solar energy and electric vehicles, these will simply be more opportunities for the private sector to innovate.

In a sense, this change in politics just highlights one of the central themes of my book. On the surface, profitability and resource scarcity may not appear to go hand-in-hand. Until, that is, you read one example after another of how innovation—creating something new with limited resources—drives business leaders to discover new value frontiers. The most valuable of these unchartered frontiers are the future values of energy, transportation, apparel, food, water, sanitation, and yet-to-be-imagined ecosystems. If the most powerful government in the world is encouraging business leaders to look away from this future, it creates all the more opportunities for clear-sighted leaders.

Many of the historical tools of progress, like scientific knowledge, journalistic facts, and critical thinking, are on shaky ground today, exacerbated by the mass production and dissemination of what passes for "information" in the media. Business leaders can choose to exploit people's confusion between fact and fiction, or they can leverage our greater access to data and powerful data analytics tools to lead their industries to create greater future value. Future first leaders can start by sifting out the real and relevant data on future trends, like the global challenges of this book. Then they can apply disciplined data analytics tools to drive their companies' strategic priorities and decision-making to turn these challenges into innovation opportunities to shape all of our futures.

One thing I've learned over the past three years that I've spent writing this book is that we cannot ever take for granted that people are good and will do the right thing. In fact, plundering, tribalism, exploitation, power blindness, and violence have always been part of the human experience. Complacency, indifference, and blatant denial in the face of these common forms of human suffering are what turn global challenges into historic global tragedies. So when people are kind and take the risks to stand up for each other, it is an act of resistance and a choice to be celebrated. And I've increasingly come to see these forms of human kindness as a gift.

The most gratifying experience of writing this book was speaking at length with many people who are committed to shaping our future for the better. I interviewed social entrepreneurs, corporate sustainability scholars, impact investors, and sustainability leaders inside big corporations. The people you've met in this book believe in their own agency to make a difference on a complex globalized planet. They're a new class of leader in a world where individuals have much less power relative to the power of economic, technical, and corporate systems. These leaders have learned how to partner with other people and systems to amplify their power to make a positive difference.

I discovered that many future first leaders have the most important "thing of value" that we can pass on to the next generation: a strong character. A strong character starts with being kind, staying true to your values, and never giving up in the face of powerful opposing forces. The next generation will need the grit, the imagination, the agency, the wits, and the perseverance to survive and flourish in the face of all obstacles and odds. This is how we can "future-proof" our children and prepare them to be ready for anything.

All of our futures, both individually and collectively, are uncertain. Life presents us with many surprising, even shocking, events and experiences. In my adult life, I've witnessed firsthand how much the world can change over a generation or two. I've experienced personally and through friends and family how anything can happen to any of us at any time. We can choose to live each day aware that none of us knows for certain what will happen next or how much time we have left. And we can choose every day which side of history we want to land on.

How do you want future generations to look back and see the impact of our choices over the next five to ten years and beyond? These choices will shape the future course of climate change, resource scarcity, and social dynamism.

Writing this book made me only more invested in the future for my kids, and for all of our kids. I see it as an imperative for the private sector to act as a powerful force for change that instills hope and a sense of agency in the next generation to determine the course of their futures. The world they inherit from us will be undoubtedly very different from the one we grew up in. It already is. But we cannot really know what global problems the next generation will face, or how they will go about solving them. We can only point them in the right direction, which is toward the multi-faceted value of the future, what's around the next bend, what's over the next horizon, and what's beyond everything we can see today. Let's have the courage to let them go there.

Acknowledgements

I have dreamed of being a published author since I could pick up a piece of paper and a pencil to write down my thoughts. For many years, I imagined that writing was a solitary act and a writer was someone who worked alone. But when I began the research for *Future First*, the first thing I noticed was how every author who inspired me had thanked hundreds of people in their acknowledgements for contributing to their books.

In the public workshops offered by The OpEd Project, I honed my desire to contribute to the world through writing. It hit home there that with privilege comes responsibility. In a writing group of fantastically smart and savvy NY alumnae from The OpEd Project, I put into practice the concept that the labor of writing is a social act.

Once I truly understood that writing a book would be a collective effort, I sought out and accepted the encouragement, advice, wisdom, and stories that people generously gave me to make this book possible.

I am deeply grateful to the more than fifty business leaders, scholars, and investors who agreed to let me interview them, graciously answering my questions and in some cases speaking with me more than once. Although not every interview was directly quoted in this book, all those conversations took me on an unexpected journey from impact investing to corporate sustainability to mission-driven business to innovation inside big and small companies. The stories, best practices, and sheer intelligence of heart and mind that so many people magnanimously shared with me on this journey are the foundation of *Future First*.

The many people I have to thank wholeheartedly for speaking with me are: Nancy Pfund, Ana Arriola, Jed Emerson, Jigar Shah, Alexander Lasky, Matt Stinchcomb, Rhys Powell, Scott Tew, Noah Murphy-Reinhertz, Kirsten Tobey, Jeanna Kimbré, Mike Brady, Andrew Hoffman, Adam Lowry, Chad Pomeroy, Joanna Lambert, Maria Blair, Julie Wainwright, Katie Orenstein, Willy Foote, Jonathan Atwood, Steve Hardgrave, the late Clayton Alderfer, James Krantz, David Kirkpatrick, Maya Chorengel, Peter Fusaro, Gabriel Thoumi, Judith Albert, Ben Bingham, Anna Snider, Edward Powers, Jennifer Barrett, Seth Weintraub, Ari Wallach, Jeff Smith, Eban Goodstein, Dawn Edwards, Irene Pritzker, Rieki Crins, Robert Rubinstein, Eric Weinheimer, Hazel Henderson, Marc Lane, Maria Fields, Jorge Newbery, Shauna Reis, Akiko Hamazaki, Octavio Dias,

Ron Klausner, Libby Bernick, Lisa Hagerman, Tanya Khotin, Stosh Cotler, and Jennifer Nadelson.

Thank you to Brooke Warner, my mentor, coach, and guide in the world of authorship, for always being the encouraging voice in my ear and the practical advisor on all things related to getting my book written and published.

Thank you to Rebecca Marsh, my publisher at Routledge, previously at Greenleaf, for believing in the message and value of *Future First* and for investing in bringing this book to market. And thank you to the publishing team at Routledge for everything they did to get my book into print.

Thank you to Nathan Means, my editor, researcher, and collaborator, for making my writing better and for making my time writing that much better spent.

Thank you to Katie Orenstein and Alex Rapson for opening the doors of The OpEd Project to us and keeping them open month after month. And thank you to Neela Pal, Lisa Kaess, and Kim Powell, my fellow NY alumnae of The OpEd Project, for your invaluable feedback, support, and competence.

Thank you to Amy Kates, my wonderful role model, colleague, and friend who has always said with her actions and words, "yes, you can."

Thank you to my parents and to my dear sisters. Thank you to all my cherished friends—you know who you are. Your kindness, generosity, and support kept me putting one foot in front of the other while writing this book.

I am ever grateful for my children, Sebastian, Julian, and Stella, for whom I wrote this book. You mean the world to me. Every day you make me want to live my dreams so that you can be free to live yours.

About the author

Alice Mann advises senior executives on how to build their leadership teams and design their organizations to achieve their mission and strategy. Mann has consulted with and coached scores of leaders of global Fortune 500 companies, preeminent non-profits, and social enterprises to inspire and deliver strong performance results.

Mann is a former vice president at JPMorgan Chase, where she led large post-merger reorganization efforts. Mann holds a PhD and MA in social and organizational psychology from Columbia University and a BA in history from Reed College, USA. Additionally, she earned a two-year organizational dynamics certification from the William Alanson White Institute. Mann has also taught a graduate course called Leading People at Columbia University. She lives with her family in New York.

Index